Ten powerful trends shaping your future

Other books by John Naisbitt

Megatrends

Re-inventing the Corporation (with Patricia Aburdene)

THE YEAR AHEAD 1986

Ten powerful trends shaping your future

John Naisbitt
and The Naisbitt Group

WARNER BOOKS

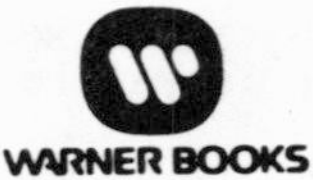

A Warner Communications Company

The Naisbitt Group; John Naisbitt, Chairman; Daniel Levinas, President.

Editor-in-Chief: Corinne Kuypers-Denlinger; Executive Editor: Jerry Kline; Director of Research: Marilyn Block.

Contributing Analysts: Pam Miller Hayes, Barbara Parry, Gale Picker, Margaret Sweeny, Pat Whittington. Research Staff: Betty Sampson, Julie Eddinger, Mark Bell, Joy Van Eldereen, Jimmy Edwards. Publications Manager: Pamela Smith Brunell.

The Year Ahead: 1986 draws mostly from the data base and publications of The Naisbitt Group, 1101 30th St., N.W., Washington, DC 20007. (202) 333-3228.

The company's publications include: The Trend Report, issued quarterly for clients; The Bellwether Report, issued monthly; Re-inventing the Corporation Newsletter, a monthly newsletter; John Naisbitt's Trend Letter, a biweekly newsletter.

Warner Books, Inc., 666 Fifth Avenue, New York, NY 10103

A Warner Communications Company

Printed in the United States of America
First Printing: November 1985
10 9 8 7 6 5 4 3 2 1

Library of Congress Cataloging-in-Publication Data

Naisbitt, John.
The year ahead, 1986.

"Mostly from the data base and publications of the Naisbitt Group"—T.p. verso.
Includes index.
1. United States—Economic conditions—1981-
2. Industry—Social aspects—United States. 3. Social prediction—United States. I. Naisbitt Group.
II. Title.
HC106.8.N35 1985 338.5′443′0973 85-17909
ISBN 0-446-38330-9

ACKNOWLEDGMENTS

This volume is the work of a number of people—the talented and diligent members of The Naisbitt Group. For their inestimable contributions to this book and to our other products, I'd like to express my appreciation and affection to each of them.

One contributor in particular deserves singling out for this work.

Corinne Kuypers-Denlinger, the indefatigable editor-in-chief for this volume and for two previous ones in this series, played an exceptional role throughout the preparation of the book. The intelligence, care, and skills that she brought from the outset—all the while performing under an extremely demanding schedule—made this book possible.

We all owe her a special debt.

Daniel Levinas

CONTENTS

The year 1986 is shaping up to be a time of important changes.

The trends discussed in this book will affect the way Americans—and people around the globe—live, work, and make money during 1986 and beyond.

Many of these changes are dramatic and pervasive—such as the social transformations created by the introduction of lasers and computers in our workplaces and homes, the surging role of innovators in the business world, and the skyrocketing importance of women as an economic force.

Other changes that we anticipate are subtle: the slow, but inexorable, global shift toward the political center, and the global movement toward private operation of traditionally public institutions, such as schools, prisons, and transit systems.

To prosper during this period of enormous changes, it's essential that we understand not only what is happening but why. New directions in social behavior don't occur in a vacuum. These trends won't suddenly erupt in 1986. In some cases, they began to emerge during the early part of this decade; in others, they became evident more recently.

The best way to anticipate the future is by understanding the present. By monitoring recent events in the retail world, for example, we can see that we're entering the dawn of the age of electronic shopping. During 1986, we believe, consumers will do a substantial amount of buying via electronic kiosks, TVs, and computer screens. Hand in hand with this retailing revolution will come merger mania and a massive shakeout among retailers—all against a background of increased competition by European retailers in the U.S. market.

The U.S. health-care delivery system, buffeted and battered by the forces of extraordinary competition, will move in two directions—toward large, centralized corporations and toward at-home self-care. American women will finally discover what advertising people and carmakers have known for years—they're an incredibly potent force in the economy and in the workplace. Young or old, in a seller's employment market, women will be courted as never before.

On the homefront, newly constructed houses will offer all the comforts—or at least conveniences—of high tech. Computers will control air-conditioning, heating, security systems. For a high-touch balance, consumers will turn to warmer, more personal styles in home furnishings.

Supported by an abundant supply of an invaluable natural resource—water—and a determination to diversify, the Great Lakes states will experience a dramatic economic renaissance. Across the nation, laser technology will ignite a job revolution, as a host of unfamiliar occupational titles—"laser spectroscopist," "gyro-optics technician," and the like—take their place beside "engineer" and "welder."

The concept of privatization—the private delivery of public services—will sweep the nation, as communities increasingly look to private enterprise to oversee education, prisons, and transit systems. Physicians, dentists, and lawyers will turn, often reluctantly, to Madison Avenue tactics to survive a market glut and plummeting prestige. In many cases, their patients and clients will benefit.

Worldwide, the emerging political trend is toward the center. From Italy to Iran, West Germany to China, a call to moderation will be heard. The reason: a growing acceptance among governments, regardless of political ideals, that the only economy is the global economy. Virtually simultaneously, a new binational corporation, U.S.A.–Japan Inc., will take its place in the vanguard of multinational corporations that operate in international markets.

Domestically and internationally, these trends add up to a period of incredible change. Those who anticipate and understand these trends will be better equipped to make the decisions of life: what to study, where to live, where to work.

John Naisbitt

1 WATERBELT STATES MAKE ECONOMIC WAVES. THE LAKES WILL RISE AGAIN.

Michigan may well go down in history as the comeback state. In fact, in the year ahead, all six Great Lakes states—Illinois, Indiana, Michigan, Minnesota, Ohio, and Wisconsin—will experience an economic renaissance that will startle traditional economists.

What magic formula will set the "Rustbelt's" economic wheels in motion once again? No magic, but there is a formula. One part water—frequently referred to as the oil of the eighties—one part commitment to economic diversity, and one part determination to act in consort, speaking with one regional voice, to reverse years of decline.

GREAT LAKES COUNCIL REDEFINES COALITION POLITICS

By the late 1970s, it had become increasingly clear that water shortages in parts of the Sunbelt threatened to bring a decade of phenomenal growth to a trickle, if not to a grinding halt. In 1981, proposals were made to transport Wyoming's coal to the Midwest via coal slurry pipelines with water tapped from the Great Lakes. Shortly after that, rumblings suggested that parts of the arid

Southwest soon would be setting up bucket brigades to drench parched agricultural land with water from the Great Lakes. In 1982, the Council of Great Lakes Governors was formed, comprising the six states named above. In addition, New York State was given voting rights on the council, although it is not a member, and a representative from Pennsylvania served on a council task force.

In February 1985, after more than two years of intensive work spearheaded by Michigan Governor James Blanchard and Wisconsin Governor Anthony S. Earl, the eight states plus two Canadian provinces, Quebec and Ontario, signed an unusual compact aimed at barring the Southwest (or any other region) from diverting the Lakes' vast freshwater reserves. Said Governor Blanchard: "This is a clear signal to the Sunbelt that we stand united to protect the greatest freshwater resources in the world."

Recognizing that the legal rules, political climate, and institutions which govern the use of water resources have changed dramatically in recent years, particularly in the United States, the Task Force on Water Diversion and Great Lakes Institutions considered several strategies designed to protect the Lakes. As a first step, the charter commits all of the participating states and provinces to follow a series of clearly defined steps over a period of years for more effective management of Great Lakes reserves.

Stating that "diversions of Basin water resources should not be allowed if individually or cumulatively they would have any significant adverse impacts on lake levels, in-basin uses, and the Great Lakes Ecosystem," the charter calls upon the states and provinces to seek legislation, where necessary, to manage and regulate diversion and consumptive use of the water. Illinois, Minnesota, Indiana, and Ohio already have laws regulating and restricting use of Lakes water. Governor Blanchard intends to ask the Michigan legislature to "enact a flat ban" on major diversions.

It is only a small step from collectively protecting the Great Lakes to collectively profiting from the sale of this region's most valuable natural resource. By the end of the decade, already thirsty regions to the south and west will be parched. Considering that the Great Lakes contain 95 percent of America's surface fresh water, and 20 percent of the world's supply, it is difficult to believe that attempts will not be made by other states to circumvent any legislative action or policy positions taken by the Council.

DRIVE TO SELL EXCESS WATER

Water "ranching" is not without precedent. Water often has been sold by federal and state reclamation agencies at fixed rates kept low by public subsidies. Complaining that the present system encourages waste by pricing water too cheaply, environmentalists and political leaders in water-short areas are prodding farmers, public agencies, and others with surpluses to sell the surplus to water-short areas, particularly fast-growing Sunbelt cities.

Small-scale water transfers already exist between the U.S. and Canada. Coutts, Alberta, for instance, has supplied Sweetgrass, Montana, with drinking water since 1963. Robert Bourassa, leader of the Quebec Liberal party, has endorsed at least a feasibility study of a $100-billion plan to turn James Bay into a freshwater lake by means of an enormous dike, and then ship the water south to the Great Lakes. From there it would be piped to western Canada and the southwestern United States. (Because Quebec has signed the Great Lakes Council charter, commencement of such a project would require approval from Council members, who undoubtedly would expect to profit from eventual sales.)

In California, water brokering is emerging as a whole new industry. By far the most ambitious project to date has been undertaken by the huge engineering firm Parsons Corp. of Pasadena. An irrigation district that owns the right to take large amounts of water from the Colorado River, as it flows through the arid Imperial Valley two hundred miles southeast of Los Angeles, has hired Parsons to undertake a conservation project. The aim is to save millions of gallons a year of water now lost through evaporation, seepage, and runoff. If successful, Parsons then will sell the rights to use the salvaged water to the highest bidder.

Another project under negotiation would have the city of San Diego buy large amounts of water from a group of Denver entrepreneurs who seek to dam a tributary of the Colorado River more than one thousand miles from San Diego. City officials say the dam would increase the volume of water flowing from the Rocky Mountains into the Colorado River and traveling south toward Mexico. For an as-yet-undisclosed price, San Diego would buy the right to draw the additional water.

Proponents of such plans argue that by adhering to a free-market principle and allowing market demands to set water prices, less would be wasted, and state and federal governments would not need to build as many multimillion-dollar dams and aqueducts. They claim these projects subsidize corporate farmers at taxpayers' expense.

Preparing to take advantage of changing market forces, the Task Force on Water Diversion already has stated that "transporting water from the Great Lakes to other areas of the country would become more feasible if water pricing policies became more realistic in regions where supplies are diminishing, or if the price of U.S. agricultural goods increased dramatically."

In 1986, the incredibly slow wheels of bureaucracy will begin grinding out pricing policies for the diversion and nonregional consumption of Great Lakes water. Make way for the water barons.

GREAT LAKES STATES CREATE AN ECONOMIC PATCHWORK

A study in contrasts, the Great Lakes states' business climate defies generalization. Although still tied to heavy industry and agriculture, both of which continue to flag under the weight of foreign competition and high interest rates, efforts to diversify some local economies are paying handsome dividends. Consequently, there has been a tremendous variation in performance between and within individual states.

Minnesota's economic base was established on the strength of manufacturing that exists symbiotically with agriculture. But during the last twenty years or so, Minnesota's industrial base has quietly given way to service, food processing, and technology businesses. With its concentration of computer hardware and software companies, Minneapolis–St. Paul ranks among the nation's major technology centers. With iron ore mining at all-time lows, the state's beleaguered Mesabi Iron Range is in sharp contrast to feverish construction activity in downtown Minneapolis. State officials hope that by encouraging tourism they can reverse the fortunes of the Iron Range.

Despite the problems of its dairy farmers and the difficulties of its machine tools and metals-related businesses, Wisconsin fared better than average among Great Lakes states when the national economy took an upswing in 1984. Economic diversity was a factor in a 4 percent increase in total employment since 1982. Ohio and Indiana had, and still have, their share of troubles, but are pulling themselves up by their bootstraps.

Ohio's bank scare put the state on the front page of America's newspapers coast to coast. Cleveland's return from the abyss of bankruptcy didn't make headlines, but it tells a remarkable story. Without the aid of Washington or the state government, Cleveland put its financial house in order. The city ended fiscal year 1984 with a $6.9-million surplus on its $239-million general budget. More than $1 billion of new construction is under way, including a forty-five-story $200-million headquarters for Standard Oil Co. of Ohio. Cleveland's port also is making a comeback. Meanwhile, to the south, Dayton has cast its lot with the military, where Wright Patterson Air Force Base, the center for U.S. Air Force research and development, employs 32,000 workers. The base's spending for payrolls, services, and construction creates a $1.6-billion-a-year impact on the local economy. As defense dollars turn over, they create another 24,000 jobs locally.

Continued anxiety over Indiana's still-ailing (and likely permanently ailing) steel industry, concentrated along the lakefront from Burns Harbor to East Chicago, can't squelch state officials' enthusiasm over Indianapolis's shimmering economic restoration. Commercial construction activity is evidence of businesses' confidence in Indiana's ability to keep its forward momentum going. Turning Indianapolis into a professional sports mecca will all but guarantee it.

In some respects, Illinois is having the most difficult time of all the Great Lakes states in reversing years of decline. Noted David Allerdice, a vice-president and economic adviser to the Federal

Reserve Bank of Chicago, in "each recessionary period, Illinois seems to ratchet down a notch in terms of manufacturing employment." He cited steel and machine tools as two of the state's glaring weak spots. On the other hand, the retail industry is booming. The MainStreet Division of Federated Department Stores Inc., for instance, opened its first three stores in suburban Chicago in November 1984 and will launch three more outlets by the fall of 1985. Meanwhile, Governor James Thompson has become a globe-trotting cheerleader for his Build Illinois program and has successfully attracted several foreign firms to the state.

By far the strongest recovery story within the Great Lakes region belongs to Michigan. Long derided as the epitome of a state in distress, Michigan has reduced its crushingly high 16.4 percent unemployment levels to 10 percent. Nonfarm personal income rose 2.5 percent in 1984, as compared to a regional average of 1.8 percent. Timber, tourism, agriculture, food processing, and office furniture manufacturing in Michigan offer evidence that the state has diversified its economy with a vengeance. Once heavily reliant on automobile manufacturing (which has picked up, but is likely to slump again), Michigan is now committed to developing its robotics industry in anticipation of a healthy economic future.

In the year ahead, the Great Lakes states will see some well-laid plans come to fruition. All too familiar with recession-induced industrial decline, and having learned some hard lessons from foreign competition, the region is preparing to meet the future. From protecting its water resources to courting foreign investments, from encouraging small business growth to advertising its recreational attractions, the Great Lakes states are focusing on long-term strategic goals, and when necessary abandoning competitive posturing in favor of coalition politics.

SMALL BUSINESSES— A KEY TO ECONOMIC GROWTH

Entrepreneurs are the engines of the new economy. More than 600,000 new companies and 2 to 4 million jobs (the majority of which are made available through new businesses) are created in the United States every year. According to Robert Friedman, president of the Corporation for Enterprise Development, a Washington, D.C.–based consulting group, "An emphasis on indigenous business creation has replaced smokestack chasing in most areas."

While the New England states were the first to develop programs to foster home-grown entrepreneurship, the Great Lakes states turned it into a fine art. All six states are making capital more easily available to new and small businesses through a mixture of public and private loans, loan guarantees, and equity investment. They're also providing expertise in business management to fledgling firms, and expanding markets for new and small businesses, especially through exporting to foreign countries. Noted Miles Friedman, executive director of the National Association of State Development Agencies: "Illinois and Minnesota have pioneered state-sponsored export programs for small business."

The state of Illinois and Chicago-based Frontenac Capital Corp., a venture-capital firm, have put $2 million each into a venture-capital pool for investment in emerging Illinois businesses. Together they are sending letters to major companies in the state, soliciting $6 million for the pool. Illinois also has launched a technology assistance program to help researchers at companies and universities get ideas off the drawing boards and into commerce, and has started a network of small business development centers at colleges and junior colleges to provide expertise and financing leads to entrepreneurial businesses. And Illinois State University in Normal has applied to be the first state school to offer an undergraduate degree in small business.

Besides providing technical assistance to small businesses interested in exporting products, Minnesota—renowned for stimulating and fiercely protecting home-grown businesses—also has created an employment development program to encourage small private businesses to hire new workers. Under the program, an employer who hires an eligible applicant gets a wage subsidy of up to five dollars an hour.

The Wisconsin Community Capital Corp., established by the Wisconsin Community Development Finance Authority, is a small business investment company with $2.5 million in capital. The organization makes equity or subordinated debt investment in start-up businesses, and the finance authority, with the aid of volunteer help from big corporations, provides management expertise for emerging companies.

Although other states have been reluctant to tap state pension funds for investment in local enterprises, Michigan has committed $100 million of pension fund assets to venture-capital projects with some link to Michigan's economy. Pension fund money will be invested in private venture-capital pools, provided the firms agree to open an office in the state. Michigan also created an Office of the Business Ombudsman, a bureaucratic troubleshooter for small to medium-sized business firms, and is encouraging a spirit of cooperation among government, labor, and business.

Before 1981, Indiana didn't have a single small-business investment company—a form of venture-capital firm created under federal law. Today Indiana is attracting national attention with its Corporation for Innovation Development. Formed two years ago with $10 million in private investments in return for state income tax credits, the corporation has opened a network of small business investment companies. To date, twenty-seven investments have been made in Indiana companies. The state also formed the Corporation for Science and Technology with a $20-million appropriation by the legislature to finance grants and loans to companies and universities for research and development.

Established in 1983, the Ohio Department of Development's One Stop Business Permit Center helps entrepreneurs deal with the maze of state regulations and requirements. The Permit Center provides comprehensive information on permits required for business start-ups, coordinates and expedites necessary permits for new and expanding businesses, and provides assistance in preparing the forms. The center also acts as a referral service to direct new or expanding businesses to technical, financial, or managerial assistance available from state agencies, universities, and local or federal agencies.

Small-business support programs are politically popular. They also pay off in tax revenues and job creation. Because a state can use its clout and borrowing power to leverage a relatively small public subsidy into a substantial pool of financial and talent resources otherwise unavailable to small and emerging business—and win public accolades at the same time—state government officials heartily endorse entrepreneurial efforts.

The Great Lakes region has learned well from its neighbors to the east. Other parts of the country will learn from the Great Lakes.

TECHNOLOGY TO MERGE HISTORY WITH HOPE FOR THE FUTURE

Frequently belittled for steadfastly clinging to its industrial past, the "Rustbelt" is about to blossom as the Silicon Valley of robotics—a sort of Automation Alley stretching from Detroit to Cincinnati. Throttled by foreign competition and reduced growth in demand for the durable goods that once marched steadily off the Great Lakes states' assembly lines, this region has embraced the manufacturers' rallying cry, "Automate, emigrate, or evaporate." Industrial automation is providing an ironic lifeline to such areas as Michigan, Ohio, and Indiana.

Initially, technological developments focus on the massive overhaul of the still-dominant auto industry (which will undoubtedly lead to even more assembly-line job losses). However, if all goes well—and most indicators suggest that it will—factories in this region soon will produce technology-based equipment for plants in many unrelated industries, ranging from appliances to electronics.

Ann Arbor, Michigan–based Synthetic Vision Systems Inc., for instance, is installing a seeing-eye computer inspection system in a Ford Motor Co. plant in Lansdale, Pennsylvania, that makes electronic modules to control emissions and perform other tasks in cars. Synthetic Vision's $1-million order backlog reflects agreements signed with Raytheon Corp., Northern Telecom Inc., and others. Said Peter Noto, company founder and president, "We can eventually inspect beer cans, lipstick, even chicken soup. We could do a food processing [inspection] machine that would be so good the government will make everyone have one."

Synthetic Vision—in which Ford invested $2 million for one-sixth ownership—is one of five machine-vision companies launched in the Great Lakes region in the last three years. Currently all of them are aimed at the auto industry, but the technology being developed can be applied to any industry that demands more precise assembly and higher quality. Such systems can guide robots and other machine tools by enabling them to see what they're doing or to recognize objects.

Robots and machine-vision systems are natural partners, so it's not surprising that robot manufacturers also call the Great Lakes states home. In fact, of roughly sixty U.S. robotics companies, nearly all, including nine of the ten largest, operate offices or plants in Automation Alley. Concentrated in Ann Arbor, the alley stretches north to Detroit and south as far as Cincinnati. Hundreds of other concerns support robot makers with facilities for writing software, with engineering talent to help install such systems, and, of course, with the machine-vision systems that are an integral component of industrial robots.

More than half the robots installed in the U.S. last year went into car plants. Although Automation Alley isn't the exclusive home of the factory-automation industry—robotics companies can be found in other areas, including Boston's Route 128, central Florida, and Silicon Valley—the alley has by far the largest concentration of robotics facilities. Said Gary Dobbs of the executive search firm Christian & Timbers in Cleveland, "You couldn't find a better microcosm of where it's all happening in robotics."

VENTURE CAPITALISTS INFUSE REGION WITH NEW MONEY

In 1982, Michigan passed a law allowing up to 5 percent of its public-employee pension funds to be used as venture capital. Some $450 million became available, making the state one of the nation's biggest venture-capital firms. Also in Michigan, the Kellogg and Dow fortunes are the major source of funds for a new Industrial Technology Institute. Some $67 million has been raised to support eighty scientists, engineers, and economists from Digital Equipment Corp., the National Science Foundation, and other big-league organizations, recruited to study the factory of the future.

Investment in growth companies throughout the Great Lakes region has skyrocketed. In the 1970s, an average of $50 million was available annually to start-up firms. By 1981, about $112 million was available to entrepreneurs. Last year, $196 million in venture capital went to new businesses or spin-offs of established businesses. Said Howard Landis, general partner in Regional Financial Enterprises, a New Canaan, Connecticut, venture-capital firm with $65 million under management: "We think it's an exceptional climate."

In early 1985, an annual venture-capital forum at the University of Michigan matched 300 investors from around the country with twenty-five new local high-tech companies. Its organizer, David Brophy, said the gatherings had led to private investments in sixty new growth companies in the Great Lakes region.

What makes this region a hot new area for investors? Several factors, not the least of which is that venture-capital markets in high-growth areas such as Silicon Valley are saturated. (A 1982 congressional study identifying this region as the area of "fastest future growth in high-tech firms" helped, too.) But more important, states in the Great Lakes region are learning how to exploit old-line industrial institutions, including, but not exclusively, well-developed universities and foundations.

Universities are becoming centers for technological research and development. A $5-million microelectronics center is being established at the University of Illinois. The University of Michigan in Ann Arbor has been turned into a first-class research center, with strong ties to the business community. For many small companies attempting to gain a foothold in the area, the university has become both customer and facilitator. Medical research in Cleveland's health-care facilities is state-of-the-art, with hospitals there enjoying a worldwide reputation. With facilities already in place, Cleveland is certain to become a center for medical biotechnology research. Wisconsin, with an excellent university system already involved in agricultural research, may well become the Great Lakes center for agricultural biotechnology research and development.

Minnesota has led the way in educational reform, including a state foundation program designed to equalize school dollars between rich and poor counties. The state has developed the nation's fourth largest public university system, and the University of Minnesota is home to one of the outstanding medical schools, which now has a cooperative arrangement with its longtime rival, the

Mayo Clinic in Rochester. The school's Institute of Technology offers pioneering programs in control systems, heat transfer, biomedical engineering, and microelectronics.

The Great Lakes region also is attractive to investors because of its built-in manufacturing facilities and know-how. As technology-based products enter the mass market consumer phase, with microcomputers becoming standard equipment in products ranging from household appliances to manufacturing equipment, an eager pool of skilled laborers will be tapped to put the items in the marketplace.

Representative of what can be expected in the future, Irwin Magnetics of Ann Arbor, which makes backup tapes for Winchester disks in desktop computers, lured away a Ford procurement executive from nearby Dearborn. When Irwin landed its first big contract with Compaq, the computer maker, it was forced to dramatically step up production. The company needed someone skilled in management of high-volume production. More companies will need similar skills. Some retraining will be necessary, and educational programs are now being put into place to address those needs.

STATES UNITE TO DEVELOP TECHNOLOGY BASE

For the past several years, competition to become the next Silicon Valley has been stiff, with each state trying to outdo its neighbors, acting independently and frequently stepping just over its borders to steal firms from neighboring states. Nine midwestern states, including some of the Great Lakes states, are bucking that trend. Working in consort, to speak with one regional voice as in the Council of Great Lakes Governors, they plan to unite under the auspices of the Midwestern Technology Development Institute.

Each member state will appoint four leaders, including educators and businesspeople, to the Institute's board of directors, and contribute $50,000 to its founding. A nonprofit policy and planning organization, the Institute is expected to establish a for-profit group of companies called the Midwest Technology Trading Corp. Later a Midwest Cooperative Technology Development Consortium will be created, linking the resources of state universities and corporations in the region.

With local research institutions already breaking new ground in every field from polymers to supercomputers, the new trading company will help universities get a fairer return in dollars, access to overseas technology, or some guarantee of participation in application of technology developed.

The idea for a cooperative effort came from Minnesota Wellspring member William Norris, chairman of Control Data Corp. (Wellspring is a public-interest group of top education, labor, business, and government leaders in the state.) Two years ago, he played a key role in launching the highly successful Microelectronics Computer Consortium (MCC), the Texas-based cooperative research effort involving eighteen computer and semiconductor companies.

GREAT LAKES STATES GO GLOBAL

According to the Japan Economic Institute, a Washington-based research agency of the Japanese government, the United States has 522 factories in which Japanese investors own a majority stake. Because these plants are geographically concentrated, the economic effect on certain areas has been particularly great. More than 350 Japanese-owned plants are located in just ten states, three of them Great Lakes states—Ohio, Illinois, and Michigan.

While Japanese-owned factories employ only about 90,000 Americans (a figure certain to soar as we move toward U.S.A.–Japan Inc.—see chapter 2), the employment impact on a few places has been substantial. Battle Creek, for example, has 500 of those jobs and will nearly double that number when Nippondenso Co. finishes a $50-million auto parts plant expansion. After Governor Blanchard headed off a labor and financing impasse that threatened to scrap the project, Mazda Motor Corp. broke ground for a $450-million auto assembly plant, expected to create 20,000 jobs in Flat Rock.

Just off Ohio's Route 33, northwest of Columbus, a large portion of Marysville's cornfields has been plowed under to make way for a new bumper crop: Honda automobiles and motorcycles. After proving that American autoworkers could successfully manufacture Japanese motorcycles—60,000 of which now roll off the assembly lines—Honda began building its popular Accord sedan at the Marysville plant. Last year, that plant reached capacity with 1,800 workers on two shifts, turning out 150,000 Accords.

Not content to rest on its laurels, Honda is expanding the automobile plant to begin building four-door Civics. Since its beginning in Ohio, Honda imported engines and gearboxes from Japan. However, Honda has changed its policy—a $35-million motorcycle engine plant has been built near the village of Anna in Shelby County, which will employ 150 workers. Honda also is building a $42-million facility near its Marysville plant to produce plastic parts for its cars. Together these projects will bring Honda's investment in Ohio to about $600 million. Employment now is about 2,600. Additionally, Honda's presence in the area has attracted a cluster of companies that sell parts to the plant, adding hundreds of other jobs to Ohio's economy.

Ohio-based companies are stepping up their investments in global product development. Procter & Gamble Co. recently introduced its newest product, Liquid Tide, which was developed in research facilities in three countries—Japan, the United States, and Belgium. Akron-based Goodyear Tire & Rubber Co. opened its International Technology Center in Luxembourg in 1957, with just three workers. Today the Luxembourg office employs 1,000 and plays a major role in company product development. Last year, Goodyear launched the first joint new-product effort between the Akron and Luxembourg offices. To facilitate the joint project, Goodyear installed direct desktop computers linking the offices.

While other states have done as well in attracting Japanese and other foreign companies to their borders, few have been more enthusiastic than Illinois Governor James Thompson. In March 1985, the governor and an entourage of 160 top labor, business, government, and academic leaders from around the state took a two-week trip to seven Asian cities. It was the largest state delegation ever to descend on the People's Republic of China. And Illinois, the nation's leading agricultural exporter, is now the first state to open a trade office there.

Although the trip's gains are still being tallied, it has already proved successful. Some contracts were signed—including one between Beatrice Companies Inc. and a Chinese company—and other firms offered letters of intent. Four Japanese firms plan to expand in Illinois as well. They are: Mitsuboshi Belting Co., Fujisawa Pharmaceutical Co., Mitsubishi Engines North America Inc., and a machine tool manufacturer, the name of which was not disclosed. The moves will entail capital investments of more than $15 million and create more than 700 jobs in the state. Upon returning from his trip, Governor Thompson remarked: "Most of the challenges this state faces are global in nature—like the strength of the dollar hurting our capacity to export. We need to turn these into opportunities whenever we can and get out there and compete."

And compete they have. Although Illinois, Ohio, and Michigan have the greatest concentration of foreign firms, the other Great Lakes states will catch up as efforts are made to tap into the global marketplace.

TOURISM GIVES STATE ECONOMIES SOME HIGH-TOUCH BALLAST

A few years ago, Indianapolis decided to replace a declining manufacturing base with a local economy based on sports. Without a major sports franchise and no prospect for one, city officials took a gamble and built the $85-million Indiana Hoosier Dome, a 61,000-seat arena. It was financed with a 1 percent food and drink tax and $30 million in charitable contributions, including $25 million from the Lilly Endowment.

The gamble paid off. Indianapolis has the former Baltimore Colts, lured there by the Dome and city promises to subsidize bank interest payments for the team's owner, and is in the midst of a recreational facilities construction blitz. New projects include a $21-million swimming and diving complex, a $6-million track and field stadium, a twenty-four-court tennis stadium, Market Square Arena (17,000 seats, costing $23 million), a $2.5-million velodrome for bicycle racing, and an expanded convention center. All of this will be capped off in the next ten years by a $200-million state park winding through the city, a $100-million downtown shopping mall, and a $48-million hotel/office complex.

Illinois's Office of Tourism has earmarked more than $14 million to promote tourism in 1985, up from $3.4 million in 1984. Ohio officials spent $3.6 million in 1984 "to stimulate growth in a growing but as yet undeveloped part of Ohio's economic base"—tourism. Governor Richard Celeste said last summer's advertising blitz was geared toward positioning the state as a weekend getaway destination for in-state and out-of-state travelers. And Flint, Michigan, is capitalizing on its automaking history to attract tourists. In July 1984, the $71-million AutoWorld theme park opened its gates. Billed as the world's largest indoor entertainment complex, with more than 300,000 square feet of attractions, the park is expected to generate at least $54 million in annual revenues.

Keenly aware of the potential danger in relying on any one sector for economic stability, the Great Lakes states have steadily diversified their industrial base. Farms and factories now abut research centers and recreational facilities, creating an economic patchwork calculated to carry the region comfortably into the twenty-first century.

2 U.S.A.–JAPAN INC. HITS ITS STRIDE. EXPLOSION OF THE NEW BINATIONAL CORPORATION.

The year 1986 will mark the beginning of the end of consumer products developed exclusively for domestic markets. U.S.A.–Japan Inc. will be in the vanguard of global corporations researching and developing consumer products for international markets. However, even as multinational ties are strengthened, there remain some troubling trade issues yet to be resolved, particularly between the United States and Japan, which are in the process of creating the first binational corporation, U.S.A.–Japan Inc.

A headline-grabbing $37-million trade deficit with Japan has captured the attention and imagination of the U.S. Congress. Accusations of unfair international trade policies—policies which many claim allow Japan to enter profitable U.S. markets while keeping their own markets closed to the U.S.—are daily fare on Capitol Hill. A host of retaliatory proposals is winding its way through the cumbersome legislative process.

Although both houses already have passed nonbinding resolutions branding Japan as an unfair trader, the likelihood of any measure with more serious ramifications becoming law is slim. In light of recent revelations, failure to act may be the best course of action. Despite the fact that Japan's tangle of bureaucracy and regulations serves as a trade barrier of sorts, international trading experts insist that on balance the Japanese government is not much less of a free trader than the U.S. or European governments, and indeed has the lowest tariffs of all industrialized nations.

By all comparable measures—including tariffs, quotas, and visible nontariff barriers such as voluntary export restraints—Japan compares favorably with other countries. When the latest negotiated tariff reductions are fully in place in 1987, Japan's average tariff on industrial imports will be 2.8 percent, compared with 4.4 percent in the United States and 4.7 percent for the European Economic Community. (When tariffs on processed food are added, Japan's average rises slightly higher than America's or the Common Market's, but is still lower than Canada's.)

Import quotas are another common protectionist method. Japan imposes quotas in twenty-seven categories, the United States in twenty-three, France in forty-six, and Britain in three. Even when voluntary quotas and discretionary licensing of imports are factored in, Japan still comes off looking less interventionist than other countries. According to William R. Cline of the Institute for International Economics in Washington, D.C., 22.1 percent of Japan's manufactured imports were subject to major nontariff barriers, as compared with 45.1 percent in the United States and 36.5 percent in France.

Some analysts assert that it is not so much the visible barriers that keep Japanese markets closed to foreign businesses, but the invisible ones. For example, William K. Krist, director of international trade for the American Electronics Association, complains that Japan's insistence on inspecting American factories and sometimes even individual products before admitting goods into Japan is a de facto barrier to trade. Because Japan often does not accept test data compiled in the United States, products must be subjected to redundant and often prohibitively expensive new tests, creating delays that most American manufacturers haven't the time, money, or patience for.

Patience, however, is the key that will unlock Japanese markets. National policies and political rhetoric aside, foreign marketers—particularly U.S. marketers—frequently fail in Japan because they simply do not understand the system. Japanese distribution systems alone are an obstacle to successful market penetration. There are many more distribution layers that must be confronted before products can be put on a Japanese retailer's shelf. And distributors there do not jump to buy products simply because they're cheaper. More important, Japanese businesspeople place a premium on long-term relationships, doing business with those who have proven themselves to be reliable partners. (Even Japanese have difficulty breaking into the market. New businesses in Japan have a bankruptcy rate six times that of the United States.)

Cultivating a long-term relationship is difficult under ideal circumstances; it can be an insurmountable obstacle for a foreigner unfamiliar with language nuances or cultural biases. One study found that a minority of American businesspeople study Japanese before arriving in that country and only 7 percent subscribe to a Japanese-language newspaper. Japanese businesspeople, on the other hand, learn our language and our way of doing business and familiarize themselves with market regulations. It shouldn't come as any surprise that they have greater success in America than Americans do in Japan.

A trade imbalance and cultural barriers notwithstanding, in the year ahead talk of protectionist measures and retaliatory posturing may well prove to be much ado about nothing as joint ventures and new business opportunities on both continents move us steadily toward U.S.A.–Japan Inc.

JAPANESE INVESTMENT IN U.S. SURE TO DOUBLE

Between 1980 and 1983 (the last year for which figures are available), Japanese investment in U.S. manufacturing facilities rose 63 percent. Judging from the dozens of projects announced since then, the total is certain to more than double in the next few years. According to the Japan Economic Institute, a Washington, D.C.–based research agency of the Japanese government, 342 companies owned or controlled by the Japanese are building or operating plants in the United States. They employ nearly 100,000 American workers. More than a quarter of those plants were not here three years ago.

Japanese manufacturers have been producing television sets and electronic components in the United States for years. More recently, Japanese firms have become fixtures in the U.S. automobile industry, in partnerships with the "Big Three" for the import of compact cars, and as onshore manufacturers of their own models. Less publicized manufacturing activities include products ranging from subway trains and elevators to tiny springs and ball bearings. The Japanese even invest in industries that Americans flee from, such as steel. They also have set their sights on participating in America's fast-growing high-tech industries, such as biotechnology, through research and development agreements with U.S. universities and corporations and through joint ventures with high-tech companies.

The Japanese are everywhere, and into everything. In Tennessee, Nissan, Toshiba, Sharp, Matsushita, and Tabuchi are now almost as familiar as Jack Daniel's and the Grand Ole Opry. The best-known Japanese-owned facility in Tennessee is Nissan's $660-million plant in Smyrna, which manufactures pickup trucks and soon will produce Sentra automobiles. Toshiba assembles television sets and microwave ovens in Lebanon. Sharp does the same in Memphis. Bridgestone (thoroughly Japanese despite its English-sounding name) produces radial truck tires in La Vergne, and Matsushita makes electronic components in Knoxville.

While some governors express reservations about the growing Japanese investment in the United States, Tennessee Governor Lamar Alexander boasts that his state, with twenty-nine Japanese companies employing 6,700 state workers, has attracted 12 percent of all Japanese capital investment in America. That Tennessee has been the most successful is, apparently, debatable. Michigan has become a mecca for Japanese automotive-related companies. Nippondenso Co. Ltd., Japan's largest auto parts supplier, recently broke ground for a $15-million headquarters and automotive research and development center, marking another step in the parade of Japanese companies locating in Michigan. Nippondenso is one of sixty-nine companies now located in that state.

One of the biggest investments by a Japanese company in Michigan, a $450-million Mazda Motor Corp. assembly plant, will be built in Flat Rock. Attracted by the proximity to auto suppliers, an available pool of skilled workers, and a $120-million incentive package from state, local, and federal sources, Mazda will break ground for the plant in 1986. Scheduled to open in 1987, it will employ 3,500 state workers.

Illinois Governor James Thompson, encouraged by the success of his neighbors to the north, went to Japan on a reconnaissance mission of his own. He came back with promises from four Japanese firms to locate or expand in Illinois, entailing capital investments of more than $15 million and creating more than 700 jobs in the state. Calling these agreements the "first fruits of his two-week investment mission," Thompson announced that he plans to visit Japan four times a year in an effort to lure new business investment to his state.

PLAYING BY THE SAME RULES

Not everyone is enthusiastic about the Japanese presence in America. Many manufacturers, who argue that products sold in the United States should be manufactured on U.S. soil, claim the Japanese do not play by the same rules as Americans—that they have created an unfair market advantage. The Japanese, they say, have dodged burdensome labor contracts and costs, sometimes by avoiding unions altogether. (Tennessee is a right-to-work state; union membership is not required to work in a unionized industry. In Michigan, Mazda Motors has embraced the United Auto Workers union, but still expects to hold its labor costs $7 an hour below Detroit's $23 average, by negotiating lower wage rates and more efficient work rules and by taking advantage of lower pension costs related to a new, younger work force.)

Others say that Japanese automobile manufacturers in the United States are American manufacturers by virtue of geography only—that their claim of 50 percent domestic content is grossly exaggerated as a result of factoring in overhead costs. Jack Barnes, Ford Motor Co.'s vice-president of corporate strategy, insists that if overhead were eliminated and only American-made parts were counted, the domestic content would be closer to 25 percent.

He may be right. American auto parts manufacturers have learned that the arrival of new automakers doesn't ensure more business. Dozens of Japanese parts suppliers are opening factories here to supply their old customers from back home. Made-in-Ohio Hondas, for instance, will have made-in-Ohio steering wheels, but they will be manufactured by Nihon Plast Co. U.S.–built Nissan vehicles soon will purchase their dashboards and radiator grilles from Lewisburg, Tennessee, but they will arrive courtesy of Kanto Seiki Co. American auto parts makers worry that Japanese auto parts manufacturers will cut into their profits by selling parts to American auto manufacturers as well as to Japanese carmakers.

For struggling smokestack industries, the issue goes beyond auto parts or domestic content. Their concern is U.S. government subsidization of foreign businesses. Many American companies resent the financial incentives lavished on Japanese rivals. A U.S. elevator industry executive said many in the elevator manufacturing industry were upset over low-interest loans and an educational grant provided by the state of Ohio to Fujitec Ltd. to locate an elevator factory in Lebanon, Ohio.

FLEDGLING HIGH-TECH INDUSTRY RESCUED BY FOREIGN INVESTMENT

Representatives of fast-growing biotechnology-based industries, on the other hand, acknowledge that without capital investment from foreign companies—with Japan in the forefront—many of them would have gone under before they introduced their first commercial product.

Amgen, a California biotech firm, had neither the money nor the marketing muscle to develop one of its most promising new products: a hormone for treating anemia. Kirin Brewery Co. Ltd., a giant Japanese beer manufacturer, had both. So the innovator with a good idea linked up with the foreign giant. Using Kirin's considerable financial resources and international distribution experience, Amgen will bring its product to market in the near future. Theirs was only one of countless such joint ventures being forged all over the high-tech world.

Ironically, these joint ventures are being consummated in an atmosphere of rising trade tensions, enabling cash-poor but idea-rich

American firms to get off the ground and multinational corporations to capitalize on their strengths and move ahead.

No estimate has been made of the number or value of such partnerships, but a Commerce Department report on biotechnology listed a sample of forty-one such relationships. Nearly half—twenty—were U.S. and Japanese companies. Most agreements involved research, licensing, and marketing arrangements for pharmaceuticals. (Biotechnology has applications in everything from agriculture to energy development, but the initial thrust has been in biomedical substances such as insulin, hormones, blood proteins, and antibodies.)

Over the past few years, availability of foreign capital was essential to the survival of this infant industry. U.S. entrepreneurs and established corporations alike quite naturally turned to Japanese investors who had both capital and well-developed international distribution channels. Even powerhouse E. I. du Pont de Nemours & Co. teamed up with a Japanese firm. Du Pont and Sankyo Co. Ltd. have formed a joint venture to market pharmaceutical products developed by Du Pont. The major advantage for Du Pont is Sankyo's "very outstanding marketing organizations," noted Jurg A. Schneider, director of product licensing in Du Pont's biomedical products department.

Japan is the second largest pharmaceutical market after the U.S. Companies hoping for a share of those sales must have a Japanese partner. Said Barry Weiner, executive vice-president of Enzo Biochem Inc., developers of a pregnancy test using monoclonal antibodies: "You need a Japanese partner to be successful in Japan—it's just the nature of the marketplace." Enzo has given Meiji Seika worldwide rights to market the test kit in return for royalties and supply contracts.

Keenly aware that present partners could easily become future competitors, some industry analysts worry that the United States—current world leader in biotechnological development—could lose that edge by sharing its technological expertise with foreign firms. But companies involved in such partnerships insist that international scientific cooperation created many of the breakthroughs that serve as the foundation of the industry and any attempt to isolate America's biotech industry would be tantamount to corporate suicide.

To a degree, technology exchange already flows in both directions. Japan perfected fermentation techniques over centuries of producing soy sauce, bean paste, and beer. The fermentation process is vital to biotechnology. In 1983, Japanese brewery Suntory Ltd. licensed technology to Schering-Plough of Madison, New Jersey, to produce gamma interferon from a synthetic gene, in what has been called the first export of biotechnology from Japan. And in 1984, a food company, Ajinomoto Co., licensed production methods of Interleukin II, a drug that enhances the immune response, to the U.S.'s Hoffman-LaRoche.

Increasingly, technology transfers are viewed as but one step in the normal course of business with a company's clients, foreign or domestic. In the end, say many in the industry, royalty and licensing arrangements will do much to bring stable profits to high-tech industries in the United States and continued leadership in world trade.

"DOMESTIC CONTENT" BECOMING PASSÉ

In 1986, the phrase "domestic content" may well pass from our international vocabulary as R&D becomes an international process for more and more companies.

Technology transfers already take place in scores of products, from consumer items to computers. Until 1982, Data General's Japanese affiliate, Nippon Data General, existed to adapt the parent company's American-made computers for customers in Japan. Then Westboro, Massachusetts–based Data General increased its stake in Nippon from 50 percent to 85 percent. At the same time, it expanded that unit's role in worldwide product development. Recently, Nippon Data General introduced the first portable computer with a screen as big as those on desktop computers. Weighing less than eleven pounds, it fits in a briefcase.

The research and development that made it possible took place in both countries. Technology for the full-size liquid-crystal display screen came out of Japan's digital watch industry. Its unique "surface mounting" manufacturing technique was developed in Japan's consumer electronics industry. (In conventional manufacturing of electronic components, each item has wire legs soldered to a baseboard. Surface mounting eliminates the legs by first gluing components to the board, then fixing them in place with soldering done partly with laser beams. Space saved allows components to be mounted on both sides of the baseboard.)

It was important to Data General that its portable computer be able to handle software designed for the IBM PC. Because the United States is ahead of Japan in software development, relevant design specifications came from Data General in the U.S. The result: a new binationally developed breakthrough in computer technology.

Not long ago, Procter & Gamble Co. introduced its new Liquid Tide. The marketing of a new detergent doesn't ordinarily make headlines, but one with a decidedly international heritage does. An ingredient that helps suspend dirt in wash water came from the company's research center near P&G's Cincinnati headquarters, but the formula for Liquid Tide's surfactants—its cleaning agents—was developed by P&G technicians in Japan. (Other ingredients, which fight mineral salts present in hard water, came from P&G scientists in Brussels.)

Because of endemic needs and conditions, certain technologies are more advanced in particular countries. Liquid Tide's surfactants were formulated in Japan because Japanese wash clothes in colder water (around 70°) than do U.S. consumers (around 95°). Surfactants must work harder in Japan to get clothes clean; consequently, that technology is more developed there.

As national differences decline in products such as computers, cars, and consumer goods, competition for product markets becomes fiercer. Businesses are opening their first research centers in foreign countries. Companies expect their overseas affiliates to do more than adapt products to local markets—they want them to be integrally involved in the research and development of new, more advanced products.

Virtually guaranteeing a U.S.–Japan research link are the number of Japanese companies that invest in American universities.

When scientists at the University of Arizona went looking for corporate money to support research on a promising medical-imaging technology—digital radiography—they made the rounds of U.S. companies they thought might be interested. They came away empty-handed. Upon exploring overseas possibilities, they struck gold. Japan's Toshiba Corp. pumped $5 million into the Arizona project in exchange for first crack at licensing any technology that comes out of that effort.

The University of Arizona's arrangement with Toshiba is not unique. Nearly every major Japanese corporation—including Nippon Telephone & Telegraph (NTT), Sony, Mitsui, and Toyota—is funding research on at least one American campus. Research links run the gamut from the development of advanced computers at Stanford University to diesel engine design at Princeton University. Noted Hiroshi Morikawa, director of science and technology at Japan's Federation of Economic Organizations: "At present, many Japanese corporations lack the ability to carry out good basic research. And through international cooperation, they can remedy what they lack."

Having turned to the Japanese in the 1970s when threatened by cutbacks in federal aid, U.S. colleges now see Japan as a major market for licensing the technology developed by their scientists. One school, Georgia Institute of Technology, has formed a partnership with a Japanese trading house to market its patented technology to companies in Japan. Nissho Iwai Corp. will have exclusive rights to sell licenses to Georgia Tech's technology in Japan, in exchange for 10 percent of any royalties. Since signing the agreement, ten Japanese companies have expressed interest in the school's technology in such areas as ceramics, electronics, lasers, biotechnology, and drugs.

Of 297 companies involved in MIT's industrial liaison program, 45 are Japanese. They include such giants as Canon, Mitsui, Hitachi, and NEC. For $30,000 a year a company can obtain first-hand access to MIT research projects. Japanese companies also have endowed nine MIT chairs at $1 million each, in such study areas as ceramics and communications. MIT officials say those contributions are dwarfed by Japanese funding of research projects in such areas as ocean engineering, materials processing, and management.

Not every university enthusiastically embraces the Japanese. Pittsburgh-based Carnegie-Mellon University, a leading center for research in robotics and artificial intelligence, prefers to meet its $52.5-million research budget with contributions from American industries. Said Angel G. Jordan, Carnegie's provost: "There is some concern on our part that this would be a transfer of technology to Japan which we should avoid." Carnegie-Mellon, however, is in a shrinking minority of U.S. colleges that turn away Japanese investment offers. As we move through 1986, the number and value of such research links are certain to escalate.

QUEST FOR MARKETS FLOWS BOTH WAYS

If it appears that U.S.A.–Japan Inc. is a binational corporation headquartered in the United States, be assured it only looks that way. Although they win fewer headlines, American corporations and entrepreneurs are beating a path to Japan's door with a determination that rivals Japan's enthusiasm for U.S. markets. So keen is American business interest in Japan that it has inspired one forward-thinking Japanese entrepreneur to start a business devoted to importing U.S. technology and creating joint ventures to help U.S. firms manufacture in Japan.

Tokyo Electron Ltd.'s (TEL) revenues shot up from $132 million in 1979 to $497 million in 1984. The enterprise counts among its U.S. clients Varian, makers of wafer fabrication equipment for semiconductors; GenRad, a biotechnology firm; Advanced Micro Devices (ADM); Digital Equipment Corp. (DEC); and Computervision.

When Varian decided it needed a manufacturing presence in Japan, it formed a fifty-fifty joint venture with TEL, called TEL-Varian. By the end of 1985, sales from the venture will exceed $50 million. ADM, maker of semiconductors, was able to penetrate the Japanese market only after teaming up with TEL. Now they are quite successful.

TEL apparently has the magic touch, particularly in sales of American electronic components to the Japanese market. In 1984, 60 percent of its sales were in semiconductor equipment, 21 percent in microprocessors and semiconductors, and 13 percent in computer systems such as Computervision's CAD/CAM workstations and DEC's VAX minicomputers.

In Japan, TEL is a rarity—a highly successful start-up company.

A growing number of footloose American entrepreneurs hope to create some magic of their own on Japanese soil. Recent changes in regulations covering foreign businesses account for this entrepreneurial tide. In 1980, the Ministry of International Trade & Industry bowed to international pressure and dropped a rule requiring non-Japanese companies to obtain its approval before opening wholly owned subsidiaries in Japan—an approval that rarely was granted. Moreover, U.S. companies that establish joint ventures with Japanese companies now have more protection over their proprietary technology.

AMERICAN SUCCESS STORIES IN JAPAN

Japanese markets are still difficult to penetrate, but a handful of Americans have had notable success. A few years ago, Henk Rogers, a thirty-one-year-old computer whiz, sought a Japanese software publisher for his video games. Only one firm showed any interest, and that was minimal. So he decided to go it alone.

Quitting his job as an English teacher in Yokohama, he founded Bullet Proof Software. The following year, its Black Onyx—a video game similar to Dungeons & Dragons—was the best-selling computer game in Japan. His company now employs thirty and aims to follow its first hit with a sequel. He has since set up a subsidiary in his hometown of Honolulu to import Japanese-style business software into the United States.

David L. Brickler, a twenty-six-year-old computer engineer, went to Japan to work for Fujitsu Ltd. After a year with the giant electronics company, he quit to try his hand as a free-lance software writer. Eventually he teamed up with a partner to form Brickler &

Elemens, which specializes in custom computer programs for business. After several years of working eighteen-hour days, Brickler now has "more contracts than we can handle."

Starting a business in Japan is difficult at best. Financing is one obstacle to success. It is all but impossible for a foreign business to get a loan from a Japanese bank or government institution. Consequently, new companies are forced to bankroll their own enterprises—costs that average between $100,000 and $500,000. Additionally, importers face prohibitive tariffs that can run to 6 percent for state-of-the-art electronics products. Perhaps the biggest hurdle American entrepreneurs must overcome is the Japanese market, which is mired in familylike business ties and cultural mores that Americans find difficult to understand. Commented John P. Stern, the American Electronics Association's Tokyo representative and a Japanese-speaking graduate of Harvard: "Most high-tech businesspeople who come to me for advice are 96 percent ignorant about the Japanese market."

In some ways, U.S. entrepreneurs are uniquely qualified to take on the Japanese market—entrepreneurs simply don't take no for an answer. They also are readily adaptable to market options. And in a country dominated by giants, there is plenty of untapped potential for low-volume custom products. Enough success stories have traveled back to the States to make Japan attractive to a growing number of entrepreneurs who find it makes more sense to compete with Japan on its own turf than to haggle over trade policies at home. Expect an explosion in entrepreneurial activity from Americans overseas.

U.S. ENTERS JAPAN'S TELECOMMUNICATIONS MARKET

Entrepreneurs aren't the only Americans invading Japan. With the announcement that Japan had agreed to drop, modify, or clarify more than half of the thirty technical standards that it demands for equipment that private users attach to its communications systems, U.S. telecommunications firms are queuing up, anxious to enter this untapped, but potentially lucrative, market. Revisions in standards will open the doors for the first time to sales of U.S.–made integrated voice-data PBXs (private branch exchanges), voice-mail machines that record and store voices in digital form, and "smart modems," which allow computers to place phone calls and transfer data over phone lines.

Previously, the Japanese government had made the decision to transform Nippon Telephone & Telegraph (NTT) from a public corporation to a private company. Industry analysts say this will do for the Japanese telecommunications industry what the divestiture of AT&T did for the American telecommunications industry. Communications companies on both sides of the Pacific should profit handsomely from these decisions.

Even before the formal announcement about altered technical standards, some American telecommunications companies quietly landed contracts with Japan's NTT, the world's second largest phone company. Chicago-based Interand Corp.—creators of the video graphics technology that allows television football announcers to diagram plays for viewers—negotiated a $5-million research and development contract with NTT. The agreement allows Interand access to NTT technology that is unprecedented for a foreign company. Pint-sized by comparison—Interand makes in one year what NTT earns in two hours—the company expects to use its access to NTT's technology to develop new communications products for international markets.

Energy Conversion Devices of Troy, Michigan, signed an $8-million contract with NTT to develop high-capacity computer memory devices. The research and development arrangement could be worth several times that amount if product developments result in the company's becoming a major supplier to NTT. And SofTech, a Massachusetts software company, won a $680,000 contract to develop technical specifications for adapting a computer language for use on NTT computers.

Not surprisingly, America's telecommunications giants also vie for a piece of the action. AT&T, IBM, and Hughes Aircraft are attempting to increase their presence in the Japanese market with a variety of products ranging from communications satellites to computers and software. Clearly, there are dollars to be made and the giants expect to earn their share.

FOREIGN BANKS FLOCK TO JAPAN'S NEWLY DEREGULATED MARKET

Japan has every intention of turning Tokyo into an international financial empire on a par with Hong Kong, London, and New York. To achieve that goal, Japan instituted sweeping liberalization and deregulatory measures that open the floodgates of global finance. Among other measures, Japan opened a highly restricted Euroyen market to unsecured foreign corporate issues and gave foreign investment bankers the right to manage such issues. Japan also moved to permit foreign banks, either on their own or in concert with Japanese partners, to get into Tokyo's fast-growing pension fund management business. (Foreign banks also were given the go-ahead to deal in previously sacrosanct secondary government bond markets.)

Furthermore, Japan authorized its banks to sell Euroyen CDs in foreign markets, freed Japanese banks and securities houses to move into each other's business, and reinforced domestic short-term markets with a flurry of lower-denomination, floating-rate money market certificates and CDs.

Japan also is considering an offshore banking setup that would exempt nonresidents from the withholding tax on interest payments and would drop reserve requirements on deposits. What's the purpose of all this? To generate more demand for the yen by making it a more truly international currency and, in so doing, to strengthen it against the dollar.

Although unlikely to dismantle regulatory barriers completely, Japan's hope is to capitalize on America's bankers' financial wizardry. Americans are pioneers in financial innovation; they possess an ability to create new types of securities and management techniques that Wall Street is certain Tokyo bankers lack.

U.S. investment banks are pouring into Tokyo. Many who have been biding their time in Tokyo for years are now building up their staffs in anticipation of frenzied activity in Tokyo's capital markets. Foreign financial outfits—mostly from the U.S.—are adding currency traders, analysts, and security dealers in large numbers in preparation for the opening of futures markets and the introduction of an offshore banking center free of reserve requirements.

Chase Manhattan Bank, for instance, has boosted its Tokyo securities and merchant banking staff from 3 to 34. Salomon Bros. has gone from 5 to 40. Merrill Lynch, which has been in Tokyo for 23 years, has a staff of 200 there. Morgan Stanley & Co. has built its staff to 111 from 35 in 1984 and plans to add another 55 by the end of 1985.

Already successful in taking a substantial share of the foreign exchange trading that shot up 25 percent when restrictions were removed, U.S. investment banks are eyeing a growing market in U.S. securities. While Japan's sizable pension fund business has a reputation of being virtually impenetrable, Chemical Bank's Tokyo office anticipates a large role for U.S. bankers as advisers. Although U.S. activity in Japan pales by comparison with Japanese activity in U.S. and other foreign markets, these liberalization measures are certain to stabilize and eventually equalize trade in financial service markets between the two countries.

From computers to cars, consumer goods to financial services, activity is strong and getting stronger on both sides of the ocean. In 1986, headlines will continue to feature trade imbalances, but the real story will be the acceleration of joint ventures between America and Japan (far more than between any other nations) as U.S.A.–Japan Inc. becomes a reality.

3 THE HEALTH INDUSTRY GOES INTO POST-SURGERY. TAKE TWO ASPIRINS AND CALL YOUR SURGICENTER IN THE MORNING.

One-third of Oregon's hospitals are in financial trouble. In Texas, forty hospitals have closed in the past two years. Across the nation, health officials estimate that up to 1,000 hospitals will close their doors by the end of the decade. And for the first time in two decades, the number of hospital beds in the United States declined in 1984.

Meanwhile, walk-in emergicenters and surgicenters—outpatient facilities, conveniently located in business districts, shopping centers, and along suburban roadways—have increased from 260 in 1981 to 2,500 currently.

America's health-care delivery system is in a tumultuous period of transition. In the past twenty years, ever-escalating costs have forced health-care givers, consumers, and those responsible for America's health-care bills—insurers, the government, and business—to ask themselves uncomfortable questions about health care in America. Not the least of the questions is: Is health care a basic human right or simply another service provided to those who can pay? If it's a right, who pays for that care when the recipient cannot?

In the year ahead, those questions will assume greater urgency as extraordinary competition moves the health-care system in dual directions: Medical Care Inc., owned and operated by large centralized health-care corporations, and at-home self-care.

HEALTH-CARE BUSINESS—A PRIVATE ENTERPRISE

Government agencies at the federal, state, and local levels recently have shown a decided inclination to turn once-public services over to the private sector. (See chapter 8 on privatization.) In most cases, the private sector has proved itself capable of performing public sector tasks more efficiently and less expensively. Although nowhere has enthusiasm been greater for the transfer of services from public agencies to for-profit institutions than in health care, the verdict is not yet in on whether private facilities will provide the same level of service to all consumers. Nor is it certain what the cost of that service will be, and who will care for the medically indigent.

A 1984 survey of 272 hospitals conducted by the Hospital Research & Educational Trust, an affiliate of the American Hospital Assn., identified no important efficiency differences between public and for-profit hospitals. An investigation conducted by the University of California at Los Angeles concluded that "given equal responsibility, accountability, and amounts of money, government-operated public services have nearly always been shown to be equal to or better than privately operated ones." Another California study found that for-profit hospital chains charged 24 percent more than public units for in-patient care. The Florida Hospital Cost Containment Board found that, during 1980–84, for-profit hospitals in that state charged 11 percent more for patient care and incurred 4 percent higher operating costs.

While efficiency and cost comparisons could well swing in favor of for-profit health-care services as large-scale medical facilities improve their managerial systems, cost savings don't explain the widespread interest in privately run facilities. But profits do. There is money to be made in health care, and in the current "let the marketplace decide" political and economic environment, the transfer of health care, like most other services, to the private sector was all but inevitable.

HEALTH-CARE CORPORATIONS BECOME ALL THINGS TO ALL PEOPLE

Among the major corporate operators, Hospital Corp. of America (HCA) was 1984's big winner, with $4.18 billion in sales. HCA was not the only corporate care giver to earn million-dollar profits. American Medical International had $2.45 billion in sales. Humana Inc. had sales of $2.01 billion, and Beverly Enterprises $1.42 billion. Although only a handful of these "supermeds" are able to turn million-dollar profits, many others also are financially strong and poised for future growth.

What's their secret? They behave like businesses, not like a public service. All are becoming health-care conglomerates, with hospitals, health maintenance organizations (HMOs), clinics, health insurers, and related groups under one umbrella organization. All are expanding, advertising, and marketing like the rest of corporate America. And, increasingly, they are gobbling up smaller, less competitive health-care facilities and merging with each other in a fast-paced race to become the General Motors of health.

Strategies to achieve that goal differ slightly. Hospital Corp. of America, the nation's largest hospital management chain, is expanding by buying up nonprofit hospitals and may soon merge with American Hospital Supply Corp., the nation's largest distributor of hospital supplies. (The merger is expected to spark other mergers and acquisitions in the country's $400-billion-a-year health-care industry.)

The linchpin of Humana's strategy, on the other hand, is Humana Care Plus, a prepaid health insurance program. Sold to employers, the plan gives enrollees a big incentive in the form of lower out-of-pocket expenses to use Humana-owned hospitals. To build a base of insured patients, Humana offers multiyear contracts that guarantee premiums will increase no faster than the consumer price index. Humana also is racing to build an empire of stand-alone, primary-care facilities, called Humana MedFirst.

One hospital in five is now owned or operated by an investor-owned health-care deliverer. Much of that growth has been in America's three fastest-growing states—California, Florida, and Texas. In Florida, 43 percent of all hospitals belong to investor-owned chains; in Texas, 36 percent; and in California, 28 percent.

Frequently condemned for eschewing expensive teaching and research facilities, health management chains now are buying, or contracting to run, university teaching hospitals. Humana Heart Institute International in Louisville, Kentucky, grabbed headlines for performing the second artificial heart operation and for promising to underwrite up to 100 of the heart procedures at a cost of $200,000 a week. National Medical Enterprises will build a $100-million medical complex for the University of Southern California, and several chains are competing for university hospitals in Houston, Irvine, California, Washington, D.C., and Boston. McLean Hospital, Harvard's psychiatric teaching facility, fought off an attempted buy-out, but soon may be operated by a hospital chain through a contractual or leasing agreement.

Hospital chains plan to turn teaching facilities into flagship and showcase hospitals. These will become keystones in a vertical integration as the chains become conglomerates that minister to every possible health need.

INDEPENDENT AND NONPROFIT FACILITIES STRIKE BACK

In an effort to combat competitive advantages enjoyed by hospital chains, independent and nonprofit facilities are borrowing a page from the chains' operating manuals. One in three nonprofit hospitals now are part of a multihospital system, association, or chain of hospitals. They cut costs and increase efficiency by buying drugs and other supplies together, sharing computer systems, and combining medical and management expertise. Some are far-reaching. One such association, American HealthCare Systems, joins 233 hospitals with 45,000 beds in twenty-one states.

Independent for-profit hospitals also pool funds to buy expensive equipment. Three Atlanta hospitals—Northside, St. Joseph's, and Scottish Rite—share the $3-million cost of installing and operating a nuclear magnetic resonance machine to diagnose a range of diseases. In Ohio, the University Hospitals of Cleveland and the Cleveland Clinic Foundation plan to copurchase a $3-million lithotripter, a four-ton machine that eliminates kidney stones without surgery.

To erase years of red ink resulting from a 67 percent drop in occupancy rates nationwide and from Medicaid's shift to a prospective payment plan, independent hospitals are closing wings, cutting staffs, freezing wages, and reducing full-time positions to part-time status. About one-fourth of Indiana's hospitals have laid off employees. Tulsa, Oklahoma's Hillcrest Medical Center trimmed its full-time staff by 400. Los Angeles's Cedars-Sinai Medical Center cut back 250 employees.

Independents and nonprofit hospitals alike also are looking for new opportunities both within the health-care field and in nontraditional areas. Denver's Presbyterian/St. Luke's Medical Center plans to build three outpatient clinics around the metropolitan area. Cedars-Sinai has started an alcohol and substance abuse unit, opened a surgical center, developed a home-care program, and expanded its rehabilitation services.

Some facilities are evolving into hybrid health-care corporations. Washington, D.C.'s Washington Hospital Center belongs to a parent company, Washington Healthcare Corp., which also has a surgicenter, a small community hospital, and an outpatient "prompt care" doctor's clinic. These enterprises are all nonprofit. However, the corporation's subsidiary, Center Properties Inc., is for-profit. It's a construction company that is currently working on such building projects as a national rehabilitation center, the hospital's garage, and a new office building for doctors.

Even more surprising is the range of non-health-care-related activities being undertaken by hospitals. A nonprofit hospital in Clearwater, Florida, has a subsidiary for-profit company that runs a printing operation, a laundry, and a durable medical goods supply company. The subsidiary provides services for the hospital at cost and to anyone else at profit-producing rates. Several nonprofit hospitals have developed for-profit hotels adjacent to their facilities to provide rooms to patients who don't need full-service hospital beds or to people visiting patients. Other hospitals, both independents and nonprofits, convert empty hospital beds to motel rooms at discount rates for relatives of patients. A survey of twenty-six hospitals in the Midwest found that more than half rented out beds for ten to forty dollars a night. Some hospitals operate laundry services, catering companies, and pizza parlors, among many other enterprises.

Such innovative revenue-enhancing tactics, say many industry observers, merely forestall the inevitable. Hospital occupancy has suffered a permanent decline. According to a study conducted by the consulting firm Arthur Andersen & Co. and the American College of Hospital Administrators, hospitals will continue to get a smaller share of the nation's health dollar. They'll receive only thirty-eight cents of every dollar spent on medical care in 1985, compared with forty-two cents in 1982.

The Andersen study also found that the number of hospitals owned or run by hospital multisystems or chains has increased 5 percent in the past five years. Today, more than 35 percent of hospitals are part of a health-care system—nearly 15 percent of those owned by for-profit chains. By 1995, said the study, most hospitals will be owned, leased, or managed by multihospital systems. Hospital administrators concur. Said Dr. John Burdine, head of Houston's St. Luke's Episcopal Hospital, "I don't believe hospitals are going to exist ten years from now that do not become part of integrated systems."

CHAINS AND INDEPENDENTS PROMOTE BUSINESS THROUGH ADVERTISING

If industry analysts are right in predicting that all hospitals will be owned and operated by multihospital systems in ten years, the next logical questions are: Which hospitals will survive the decade and how will hospitals guarantee survival? Diversification is proving to be one answer. Another tactic being taken by both independents and chains is to behave like a business—actively recruit customers and guarantee satisfaction.

Columbus Hospital, in the Chicago area, offers patients a money-back guarantee. Inaugurated in response to increasing competition, the guarantee offers patients refunds if they or their doctors are dissatisfied with the hospital's services. Said George Purvis III, chief operating officer, "We cannot guarantee the results of medical treatment, but we can guarantee complete satisfaction for services such as nursing care, meals, waiting time for testing and results—in fact, for any and all services the hospital provides." Such a guarantee is unusual, but not unique. Blanchard Valley Hospital in Findlay, Ohio, for example, has been guaranteeing its services since 1974.

Dallas-based Republic Health Corp. now sells its services like Chrysler sells cars. Republic relies on heavy doses of promotion. "Step Lively" is its latest marketing slogan. In an effort to lure people with foot problems to seek surgery at Republic's General Hospital at Lakewood, Texas, the company has launched a newspaper campaign. Promising reduced rates for foot examinations, a free take-home meal after surgery, and a $20 gift certificate toward a new pair of shoes, Republic hopes to fill some empty beds. A "Gift of Sight" promotional blitz conducted by a Republic hospital in Southern California promised to absorb deductibles—$356 for patients with only Medicare insurance—and gave $50 gift certificates toward new pairs of glasses. Two thousand people responded to the advertisement; 100 were operated on.

Opening for business in 1981, Republic started with eighteen facilities cast off by HCA. Labor costs were cut by increasing part-time employment and getting full-time workers to do more tasks. Republic eliminated service duplication by funneling all the business for certain treatments to one hospital in each service area. By keeping an eye on the bottom line, and the company in the public's consciousness, Republic has enjoyed healthy growth. Revenues in the first half of 1984 reached $264 million, compared with $211 million for all of 1983. Earnings rose to $9 million, more than double those for all of 1983.

Republic is not alone in relying on media campaigns to reach new customers. In 1983, Denver's Presbyterian/St. Luke's Hospital had no advertising budget. In 1984, it spent $500,000, and in 1985 its advertising budget totaled $1.2 million. Special deals are being offered by a growing number of health-care facilities. In a mass mailing to area residents, Maryland's Carroll County General Hospital sent out $2-off coupons for treatment at its outpatient clinic.

A task force created by Minnesota Governor Rudy Perpich is studying ways to turn the state into a health-care center. Borrowing an all-inclusive package concept from the travel industry, the task force puts together health-care packages for out-of-town patients. A Georgia business executive in need of chemical-dependency treatment, for instance, could be sent with his family on an "all-inclusive treatment package" to Minnesota. The executive's family could live in a hotel, eat in the hotel dining room, and use a rental car for sight-seeing while the executive receives care at one of the state's large treatment centers—all for a prearranged price that includes round-trip airfare on a Minnesota-based airline. Interesting idea.

Not surprisingly, such tactics have led to price wars in some areas. When the occupancy rate at Phoenix's Valley View Community Hospital plunged to 33 percent as a result of stiff competition from neighboring hospitals, Valley View slashed prices. Emergency room rates dropped from $100 to $29. Outpatient cataract surgery was reduced from $545 to $420. Face-lifts, usually $1,700, cost $440.

In the year ahead, we can expect to witness already fierce competition grow even more intense as hospitals compete for an ever-dwindling supply of inpatient customers. Creative strategies aside, life-style changes and the availability of cost-effective, efficient, and high-quality outpatient care—combined with greater reluctance on the part of employers to finance hospital care when alternative care would do as well—are encouraging more and more Americans to avoid hospitals altogether.

McDOCTOR'S AND DO-IT-YOURSELF CARE ALTER THE INDUSTRY

Walk-in emergency clinics and outpatient surgery centers are transforming the business of medicine. A 1983 study by the Orkand Corp. of Silver Spring, Maryland, projected revenues of $2 billion to $2.5 billion for the industry by 1990. According to the study, average industrywide profits in 1982 were about 13 percent of revenue, with patient volumes growing 20 percent annually. Emergicenters have grown from 260 in 1981 to 2,500 currently. And the Dallas-based National Assn. for Ambulatory Care expects 3,000 clinics to be operating by the end of 1986.

Ownership of the clinics is about evenly divided between multi-hospital corporations, like Humana, and private physicians and hospitals. Many industry analysts are convinced, however, that in time clinics, like hospitals, will be part of health-care conglomerates under the protective wing of such corporations as Humana, HCA, and Beverly Enterprises. For now, freestanding, independently owned emergicenters and surgicenters are giving the chains a run for their money.

Falling loosely into two categories—ambulatory surgical centers for routine, nontrauma surgical procedures, and emergency-care centers for minor medical problems such as earaches and broken bones—the centers are a cross between private physicians' offices and hospital emergency rooms. Located in or near shopping centers, and demanding payment on the spot, these clinics offer convenient service at 40 to 80 percent less than hospital or private physician fees.

With proliferation of the centers has come increased criticism. Referring to such clinics as "Doc in the Box" or "7-Eleven medicine," critics express concern that because many centers don't have blood banks, laboratory equipment, surgical rooms, or monitored intensive-care beds, the use of "emergency" in their title is misleading and even poses a life-threatening danger to consumers. Proponents counter that clinics are capable of stabilizing seriously ill patients and do not hesitate to transfer trauma cases to hospital emergency rooms.

Criticism has done little to dampen consumers' enthusiasm. Emergicenters and surgicenters annually treat some 45 million patients nationwide, earning revenues of $1.8 million. Asserting that the ambulatory-care industry is a "marriage between business and medicine," James R. Roberts, executive director of the National Assn. for Ambulatory Care, states that the ambulatory care industry "is going to cause intensified competition across the board ... freestanding medical clinics are the gatekeepers to the overall health-care delivery system in the future."

Competition will indeed intensify, particularly as the already pervasive wellness movement gathers momentum, embracing ever-growing numbers of Americans who would just as soon treat themselves as go to a physician, hospital, or other health-care facility.

The market for medical self-care is a booming industry. Americans are learning the value of eating right and exercising regularly. A recent poll indicated that 59 percent of adult Americans said they exercised daily—up from 24 percent in 1964. Low-fat milk accounted for 18 percent of all milk sold in 1970; by 1980, the share had risen to 37 percent, according to the U.S. Department of Agriculture. Decaffeinated coffee accounted for 6 percent of all coffee sales in 1970. In 1980, it was 20 percent.

A 1984 survey by the Proprietary Assn. found that most common health problems are never seen by a doctor. Interestingly, self-care increases with income and education. And a large part of the self-care market consists simply of information. Circulation of the seventeen major health-related magazines jumped from 3 million in 1970 to 7.4 million in 1982.

Probably the oldest and largest segment of the self-care market involves vitamins, nutritional supplements, and "health foods." According to the Council for Responsible Nutrition, sales of nutritional supplements in 1984 totaled $2.6 billion. Although there are some giants in this market segment—American Cyanamid (makers of Stresstabs), Warner-Lambert (Myadec), Miles Laboratories (One-A-Day), and Squibb—industry leaders control only a fraction of total sales. Most sales are earned by private label firms that sell door-to-door or by mail order.

An important and rapidly growing segment of the self-care market is home diagnostic kits. Most familiar in this area are home pregnancy test kits, currently with sales around $40 million annually and expected to rise to $57 million in 1987. A leader in this field, Personal Diagnostics of Whippany, New Jersey, earned $1.2 million in 1983. Personal Diagnostics is now developing tests that use disposable microprocessors to detect fertility in women and a host of conditions including pregnancy, diabetes, urinary tract infections, and strep throat.

As more people jump on the fitness bandwagon, encouraged by

employers' incentives to workers who stay out of the doctor's office, the self-care industry will continue to grow.

ETHICAL QUESTIONS TAKE ON URGENCY

Business spending on health care in 1984 was almost equal to after-tax corporate profits—around $90 billion, almost double the amount spent in 1980. Sixty-nine percent of the population has employer-provided health insurance, with the employer typically paying about 80 percent of the premium. (Efforts in recent years to put more of the cost burden on employees, through higher deductibles and by asking them to pay a greater proportion of health insurance upfront, is bringing that percentage down slightly.) At the same time, 35 million Americans have no health coverage of any kind, and Medicare and Medicaid pay a steadily diminishing fraction of health services for the elderly and the poor.

With guaranteed payments for any treatment, the medical community once was free not only to charge whatever the market would bear but to pour funds into ever more sophisticated technology. Some industry analysts estimate that as much as 40 percent of the annual increase in health-care spending in the 1970s was attributable to technology. Total spending on health care rose from 4.4 percent of the gross national product in 1955 to 11 percent in 1984. While increases have slowed somewhat in the past two years, America's annual health bill remains exorbitant.

Cost containment became the national rallying cry at the beginning of the decade, and the din has yet to subside. Meanwhile, a second issue has been introduced—one that was generally overlooked at a time when universal access to high-quality health care was already a given. It is a question of ethics. If costs are to be contained, then expensive equipment and surgical procedures must be used judiciously. Who decides what constitutes an appropriate application of technology, and, once decided, who pays for its use?

Although all agree that something must be done, only a handful of experts have stepped forward to suggest that health care should be—and, insist some, must be—rationed. Dr. William B. Schwartz, professor of medicine at Tufts University, who conducted a study of the problem at Brookings Institution in Washington, D.C., said: "The only way to cut costs will be to deny benefits to some people or deny benefits for some diseases." Colorado Governor Richard Lamm created a national stir, and triggered countless debates, when he said that we're spending too much money to keep terminally ill elderly people alive.

Some suggest that the United States should consider following in Britain's footsteps. Certain health-care procedures there are stringently rationed. For instance, two-thirds of British patients with kidney failure are denied dialysis. By contrast, virtually all kidney patients in the United States are treated, at a cost of nearly $2 billion a year.

In some respects, health care already is rationed. Medicare and Medicaid now pay according to diagnostic-related groups, which specify a flat fee for more than 400 procedures. If hospital costs for treatment rise above those limits, the hospital pays the difference. If costs fall below, hospitals keep the difference. Many analysts insist that health-care administrators closely monitor treatment in an effort to hold down expenses. In effect, corporations, too, are forced into the role of medical policymakers. Although none openly refuses to pay for such expensive procedures as heart and liver transplants or coronary bypass operations, approval must be granted on a case-by-case basis by company medical directors (not necessarily persons with medical degrees).

No one is stepping forward to make decisions on appropriate care. Doctors argue that they are obligated to take whatever steps are necessary to save lives and that decisions about accessibility of health care must be made by policymakers. Meanwhile, policymakers argue that doctors are the only ones able to decide what is reasonable care and to take steps to limit the use of costly technology themselves.

Deciding where to draw the line will be a painful process. There is, however, a contingency that in the year ahead will become more of a factor: Americans are asking state legislatures and courts for the "right to die." By 1985, twenty-eight states had passed legislation giving legal validity to the "living will," a statement made by competent persons about what they want done in the event they become incompetent to make decisions about their own medical treatment.

Courts in many jurisdictions honor living wills and permit the removal of respirators from comatose patients. Since the landmark ruling in New Jersey in 1976, in the case of Karen Ann Quinlan, judges have recognized a person's right to die with dignity.

Furthermore, physicians increasingly recognize that along with their obligation to preserve and prolong life is another equally valid goal of medical practice: the relief of suffering. Although these two goals often conflict, there seems to be greater willingness on the part of physicians and other medical practitioners to at least consider the wishes of the patient and the patient's family in determining level of care.

In 1986, the "right to die" movement once again will put the issue before state legislatures and test the issue in courts around the country. Quality of life is replacing quantity of care for many. In the end, decisions about whether life-sustaining procedures should be continued or terminated will be left up to the individual. Cost will continue to be an issue, but it's unlikely we'll see an endless line of terminally ill people anxious to be hooked up to expensive technological equipment that can maintain, but not enhance, life.

4 IT'S A WORKING WOMAN'S WORLD IN A NEW SELLER'S MARKET. THE ADVANTAGE SHIFTS.

Women have developed the Midas touch. While everything they touch may not turn to gold exactly, every work arena they enter undergoes a dramatic transformation. Since the early 1970s, women have been flooding into the work force. Not content to remain forever in female-dominated job "ghettos," women have donned hard hats and helmets, lab coats and judges' robes, and have picked up scalpels and sledgehammers. In doing so, they have permanently altered society's precepts about women's work and men's work.

In the year ahead, women and men will realize what advertisers and public relations people have known for some time—women are reshaping the marketplace. Also in 1986, labor shortages will create a seller's market for jobs. Women will be courted by corporations whose doors, until now, have been closed to them. In the coming seller's market, it will be a woman's world.

WOMEN MOVE INTO THE WORKPLACE IN RECORD NUMBERS

Seizing two-thirds of the jobs created in the past decade, women have become a powerful economic force (and, consequently, a political force) in their own right. Nearly 50 million American women are in the work force—around 53 percent of women over sixteen who are capable of working, and 45 percent of total employment. By 1995, six of every ten American workers will be female.

Already, the female labor-participation rate in the United States exceeds that of almost all industrialized nations—surpassed only by Sweden, where the rate is about 80 percent. In Japan, the proportion of the female population at work has actually dropped since 1970, from 49.3 percent to 47 percent. And in West Germany, the female participation rate has held steady for the past decade at 38 percent.

For the most part, women remain in lower-paying clerical and service jobs—teaching, waitressing, nursing, etc.—but they're gaining ground in formerly all-male preserves.

A confluence of circumstances makes it possible for women to enter male-dominated jobs.

In some cases, job demands have changed with the introduction of technology. In the insurance industry, for example, claims adjuster and examiner positions were held by men who were expected to spend their time away from the office, inspecting dented fenders. Today the same tasks are accomplished with a computer terminal. Women now hold 65 percent of these jobs—up from 27 percent in 1970. Automatic machines for moving sides of beef in the meatpacking industry eliminated the need to lift hundreds of pounds of meat and opened the way for women to take such jobs. Since 1970, the proportion of packinghouse butchers who are women has increased by more than one-third.

Higher levels of educational achievement are making women attractive candidates for executive positions and give women the tools they need to enter the professions. Women earned 28 percent of the M.B.A. degrees awarded in 1982. (In bellwether Florida, 47 percent of the business students at the University of South Florida are women.) In 1980, 14 percent of lawyers were women and 12 percent of doctors. By 1984, women represented 16 percent of both professions. In the year ahead, those percentages are certain to increase as a third of all law students, and more than a fourth of all medical students, are now women. (In some of the nation's most prestigious professional schools—Stanford, Harvard, and Yale among them—women make up 50 percent or more of the student body.)

Today, professional and executive occupations are considered sex neutral. Accounting and auditing, banking, computer programming, personnel, and property management positions are filled by women as well as men—not in equal numbers, but women are beginning to catch up.

JOBS FOR THE INFORMATION EXPLOSION

As America makes the transition from an industrial economy to an information economy, new jobs are created by the hundreds of thousands each year. Many of those positions are designed specifically to handle the information explosion. Most require good reasoning skills, an aptitude for math, and excellent interpersonal skills. At almost every level, from taking airline reservations to monitoring hospital intensive-care units, the single most important job requirement is literacy. And for the first time in the history of the United States, women are better educated than men—women now account for 52 percent of all college undergraduate enrollees.

By no means have women replaced men in the work force. Men are still a solid majority—56 percent of all workers. Nor have women taken jobs away from men. What they have done is improve their competitive edge.

In 1986, that edge will become even sharper as women outpace men in entering the work force and as female entrepreneurs become an ever more important cog in America's incredible job-creation machine. Every year, some 600,000 new companies are created in this country. Nearly one-third of those companies are started by women, and they account for $40 billion in earnings.

Despite impressive gains, women still confront job-related sex discrimination and are nowhere near income parity with men. In the year ahead, we will witness the beginning of a turnaround. Already-serious labor shortages will become critical shortages as the baby-boom generation (all 60 million of which have, miraculously, been absorbed into the labor force) gives way to the baby-bust generation. From now to the end of the decade and beyond, the available pool of young workers will continue to shrink. Continued economic growth will lead to the creation of 2 to 3 million new jobs every year. Meanwhile, fewer than 1.5 million new workers will enter the labor force. Protracted labor shortages will result.

After years of enjoying a buyer's market, employers will face a seller's market. Workers of all ages and both sexes will be courted as never before. What the government, in all its ponderous bureaucracy, has so far been unable to accomplish (except in a handful of states), economic necessity will accomplish in short order: equal pay for work of comparable value. And furthermore, the last vestiges of sex discrimination will begin to fade away as employers seek to attract and keep the person best qualified for the job.

CORPORATE AMERICA AND OTHERS RALLY IN SUPPORT OF WOMEN

In early 1985, Mobil Corp. placed ads in a variety of business publications requesting other corporations to follow its lead in making donations to the American Woman's Economic Development Corp. (AWED). Formed in 1976 with a federal grant to develop a model program of entrepreneurial assistance for women, and working with faculty at the Harvard Business School, AWED identified management training and technical assistance as the most useful tools for women beginning their own businesses.

AWED developed a program that included: group sessions for women who know what business they want to enter, but need help in learning how to go about it; an eighteen-week training and counseling program for new entrepreneurs; an eighteen-month management training and technical assistance program for women who have been in business for at least a year; a two-year training program for women whose businesses gross more than $1 million annually; and a counseling hot line.

More than 26,000 women have participated in one or more of AWED's workshops—18 percent of those trained and 25 percent of those counseled by the organization were minority women. Among program participants since 1977, less than 1 percent subsequently declared bankruptcy. Said the Mobil advertisement: "AWED doesn't benefit just entrepreneurial women. It benefits the people they hire. And it helps to produce millions of dollars in tax revenue."

Other corporations apparently share Mobil's attitude toward helping women succeed. Minnesota Mining & Manufacturing Co. (3M) is concerned about a nationwide shortage of scientists. The company decided to do something about it. Through its unique program called the Visiting Women Engineers and Scientists Program, 160 women employed in scientific specialties at 3M are sent around the country to interest female high school students in majoring in chemistry, biology, and engineering. (While the 3M scientists are visiting high schools, another group is off on a similar mission at the college level, urging female students to major in chemistry. A consortium of five colleges has formed a program to stimulate interest in science among undergraduates.)

Over the past ten years, IBM has supported more than ninety programs designed to strengthen women's skills. It has created small grants for precollege programs in engineering, awarded major grants for science programs at leading women's colleges, and established foundations to finance doctoral fellowships in physics, computer science, mathematics, chemistry, and engineering.

For the last five years or so, a number of U.S. corporations, such as Borg-Warner Corp. and Equitable Life Assurance Society of the United States, have created in-house networks to help women employees move up the corporate ladder. In an interesting twist, some businesses are reaching beyond their own organizations to help networking organizations within the community. Anheuser-Busch Companies Inc., the $6.5-billion brewing conglomerate based in St. Louis, Missouri, recently gave $27,000 for the first national conference of the 2,500-member National Network of Hispanic Women, based in Stanford, California.

Made up of fifty community businesswomen, the Professional Women's Network in Rosemont, Illinois, is supported, in part, by the Northwest Commerce Bank of Rosemont. Started in 1984, the network has cost the bank $25,000 so far. Nice gesture. Even nicer, the program is not limited to bank employees or customers. Any female executive or small-business owner in the community can participate in its seminars and workshops, take advantage of special bank services, including use of its computer, and benefit from the encouragement and advice of other members.

Private nonprofit organizations also are cropping up around the country in support of small-business owners, particularly low-income women. One such program, HUB Program for Women's Enterprises, based in New York City, developed a strategy by which it was able to identify women who owned their own businesses or wanted to become self-employed but needed help. Targeting Hartford, Connecticut, as its model, HUB (its director, Jing Lyman, chose the name because "women are at the hub of economic revitalization in their communities") sought contributions from area corporations, a local bank, and foundations.

Program sponsors are not likely to be disappointed. Robert E. Sadler, vice-president of the Greater Hartford Chamber of Commerce, said officials estimated that their initial investment of $83,000 would, in ten years, generate $43 million annually in new business income and create 890 full-time and 500 part-time jobs. Appears to be a sound investment. Similar programs are planned for Philadelphia, Newark, and Flint, Michigan. Sponsors hope the program will become a model for other communities.

EDUCATION AND TRAINING GIVE WOMEN A LEG UP

When information is the strategic resource and people are any company's principal asset, access to appropriate educational programming becomes critical. Women are enrolling in colleges and universities in record numbers. They're also flocking to education and training programs designed specifically for their special needs and interests. Academia is responding to consumer demand by creating new, innovative courses for women.

The Simmons College Graduate School of Management in Boston does something it says no other institution in the country does: It offers women a shorter, more intensive master's of business administration (M.B.A.) program that emphasizes survival skills for male-dominated executive suites. Sensitivity to women's needs sets this program apart. Night sessions are offered, and women without college degrees are accepted if they can pass the entrance exam.

Begun in 1974 in an unused typing room at Simmons, with an initial budget of $12,000, the program now is housed one mile from the main campus in an elegant town house. Simmons spends $1.3 million annually to administer the M.B.A. program and a ten-week middle-management course.

Apparently the program is a success. A survey of the first class of 32 students (the current class has 182 students) revealed that graduates earn an average salary of $70,000 a year. More than a third of that first group earns more than $100,000 annually. Graduates work in all sectors of business and industry. Since its inception, Simmons has added courses in career planning and computer planning, and now boasts a job-placement bureau. Corporate America has expressed confidence in the middle-management program by paying employees' tuition costs. Among the companies that have put employees through the program are Xerox Corp., Hospital Corp. of America, General Motors, Avon Products Inc., and Continental Illinois National Bank and Trust Co. of Chicago.

Another innovative program, developed by Missouri's Department of Elementary and Secondary Education vocational services office, offers area women training opportunities in nontraditional fields. Believed to be the first of its kind in the country, the Women in Nontraditional Careers program attempts to address the needs of rural women while taking advantage of the growth in high-tech areas. Attracting nationwide attention, the program so far is offered on three college campuses: East Central College in Union, Mineral Area College in Flat River, and Jefferson College in Jefferson Parish.

Courses of study include machine-tool technology, robotics programming, construction, air-conditioning and refrigeration technology, and agribusiness. Up to 100 percent financial aid is available for students in need. The program also offers guidance, counseling, scheduling, and referral services for women interested in pursuing careers in male-dominated professions. Women are referred to whichever campus offers the best training in their chosen fields. Enrollment has tripled since its inception, and program administrators expect continued growth.

For two years, the nonprofit Women's Computer Literacy Project (WCLP) has helped women overcome job-limiting "technofear." Thousands of women in New York and San Francisco have paid $265 for a two-day session that helps them become more familiar with the operation of a personal computer and make sense of an instruction manual, and provides them with guidelines to become intelligent consumers. WCLP's founders prefer all-female classes because apparently women are easily intimidated by technological jargon and few are encouraged in their academic careers to pursue highly technical classes. A precept of the class is that women must overcome their fear if they are to keep their jobs or move on to higher-level positions.

The Mary Ingraham Bunting Institute of Radcliffe College in Boston is one of the five largest centers in the country awarding postdoctoral fellowships, and the only one primarily for women. Although some of the forty fellows are researching women's issues, the common thread among Bunting scholars is that they are women, not that they study women's issues. Students from across the country and several from abroad study full-time, living on a stipend of $15,000 to $16,000. Funding comes from the Radcliffe endowment, private foundations, and, in some cases, federal research offices.

Originally created to meet the needs of educated married women who could not study full-time because of family responsibilities, the institute now provides fellowships to single women as well. Fellows aver that the institute is a special place because, as one put it, the school offers "a kind of intellectual and emotional freedom and support [women] seldom find in the male-dominated outside world."

UNIONS COURT WORKING WOMEN

In the past decade, unions have experienced a dramatic and potentially terminal decline in membership. Attempting to reverse their fortunes, unions have been actively recruiting women—quite successfully. Today, one of every three members is a woman. Accounting for more than half the total increase in membership in the past twenty years, more than 7 million women belong to unions, up from 4 million just a decade ago.

Although union representation is spotty, and winning new members is increasingly difficult, over the past five years, the Amalgamated Clothing and Textile Workers Union won representation elections covering 2,000 workers in Colorado—75 percent of them women. They gained members by embracing concerns unique to working women, including the issue of equal pay for work of comparable value.

Female union members also are organizing from within to guarantee continued union support of women's issues. Ten years after its founding by 3,000 union women, the Coalition of Labor Union Women has grown from ten chapters to seventy-five around the country. It has 18,000 dues-paying members, a membership that includes the rank and file as well as international vice-presidents.

Not content with rank-and-file membership, women are assuming union leadership roles. Until 1980, no woman had ever sat on the AFL-CIO's executive council—the federation's key policymaking group. Today, two women sit on the council. In 1983, Teamsters president Jackie Presser named Vicki Saporta head organizer of the 1.9-million-member union. A graduate of Cornell University's School of Industrial and Labor Relations, Saporta was the first woman ever to hold that post. About 350,000 female truck drivers, clerical personnel, health-care workers, and flight attendants have since joined the Teamsters.

Vicki Saporta and Karen Nussbaum—president of 9 to 5, the National Association of Working Women, an affiliate of the Service Employees International—are among the growing number of women rising to union leadership positions. The secretary-treasurers of four major state labor bodies now are women. Several women have served, or currently serve, as president or secretary-treasurer of more than 100 regional union councils and have held the presidencies of hundreds of local unions.

Unions are learning that if they are to survive the transition from an industrial economy to an information economy, they must be responsive to women's concerns. Said Pat Scarcelli, recently appointed director of the Women's Affairs Department of the 1.3-million-member United Food and Commercial Workers Union,

"Women will probably be the most important factor determining the fate of the labor movement in coming years. Our challenge today is to organize the new service industries—real estate, insurance, finance, and others—where there are concentrations of women." She's right. To ignore half the labor force would be a fatal mistake.

WOMEN IN POLITICS: GET READY FOR MS. PRESIDENT

Geraldine Ferraro may have grabbed headlines for her first-in-the-nation vice-presidential nod, but it's at the state and local levels that women have steadily gained prestige and power. Women are building a foundation in city halls, courthouses, and state houses for generations of voters to come, for whom gender will be a nonissue. It will not be long before a woman delivers the State of the Union address.

Forty-three women currently hold top statewide elective offices. Included among them are the governors of Kentucky and Vermont and U.S. senators in Florida and Kansas. Five women serve as lieutenant governors, eleven as secretaries of state, and eleven as state treasurers. Women hold mayoral offices in ninety cities with populations greater than 30,000. And in 1984, women gained 100 seats in state legislatures across the country, for a total of 1,096—15 percent of all the state seats, up from 8 percent in 1975.

A historic revolution is occurring. Not only are women gaining political office via the ballot box, they are winning recognition as an important party power base. Consequently, women are being appointed to top state leadership positions in record numbers. Women now hold almost 20 percent of all top cabinet-level positions, and in several states as much as 40 to 50 percent. With each state election, the number of women elected and appointed to top-level positions grows.

Adopting the philosophy that "money is power, learn to ask for it," women's political organizations are becoming more aggressive in their campaign-funding tactics. At the same time, women voters show a greater willingness to loosen their purse strings in support of female candidates.

An already well-developed power base will grow stronger as women become better able to organize, finance, and choreograph campaigns at the local, state, and national levels. A principal goal of the Women's Campaign Fund (WCF) is to increase the number of females in national office. In 1986, the WCF plans to recruit only in districts where female contenders have a good chance of winning and then train them in special candidate schools. Said Donna Marshal Constantinople, a member of the board, "We are looking for races that will yield the highest return on our investment, which was one of the hardest lessons we learned in the '84 campaign."

It was a lesson well learned. Of the sixty-five female candidates for House seats, only two newcomers joined twenty incumbents. Most of the losing female candidates were little more than political sacrifices, pitted against incumbents regarded as unbeatable. The year ahead will witness a dramatic shift in strategy as female politicians walk through the door opened by Geraldine Ferraro. As early as 1988 we are likely to see a female-led presidential ticket, and quite possibly a string of Ms. Presidents thereafter.

ECONOMIC GAINS RESHAPING THE MARKETPLACE

In recent years, economists have fretted over the shrinking middle class, asserting that if economic patterns continued, the middle class would disappear. It hasn't and it won't. With aggregate earnings of $500 billion annually, working women are guaranteeing its continued viability.

According to a study conducted by the Conference Board, the influx of women into the labor force is a major reason why 46 percent of all families now earn more than $25,000 a year (in today's dollars), compared with only 28 percent two decades ago. In families earning $10,000 to $15,000, only one-third of the wives work outside the home. Two-thirds of wives in families in the $30,000 to $35,000 range bring home paychecks. And in families with incomes between $40,000 and $50,000, 70 percent of wives are in the work force. Said

Conference Board consumer economist Fabian Linden, "An impressive 60 percent of all family income is now earned by households where wives are working."

While women's economic contribution is significant, the picture is not all rosy. Women's pay, as mentioned earlier, still does not equal that of a man's in the same position, nor in jobs requiring a similar degree of skill and training. Although gains have been made—women now earn 64 percent of what men earn, a figure that will increase to 74 percent by the year 2000, according to Santa Monica, California–based Rand Corp.—income parity has yet to be achieved.

Nevertheless, women are earning greater respect as an economic force to be reckoned with. Consequently, an ever-increasing range of service industries have turned into growth industries as the marketplace scrambles to meet the needs of working women. Day-care centers and training schools for nannies are springing up around the country. Maid services are more widely available. Realtors and builders are keenly aware of the growing female market for homes and condominiums. Carmakers and distributors now view thirty-four-year-old single professional women as a major market. And before long, retailers will follow Carson Pirie Scott & Co.'s lead in creating complete specialty stores for working women.

The importance of working women to the U.S. economy, already enormous, will escalate over the next few years. Preparing for and responding to marketplace demands for appropriate support programs and services represents a golden opportunity for entrepreneurs and established corporations with foresight and vision. What's more, when women are accommodated, everyone benefits.

5 SMART BUILDINGS, SMART ROOMS CHANGE THE WAY WE LIVE AND WORK. IT'S WHAT'S INSIDE THAT COUNTS.

When visitors come to view builder Ron Watson's new three-bedroom home in a Dallas suburb, they are greeted by a mechanical voice that announces, "This is Watson speaking. The front door is open." The Watson that is speaking is not Ron, it's a computer—a sort of electronic watchdog that Ron Watson built into the custom-designed home. At present, Watson—the computer—looks after the house's security system, but soon it will be programmed to control interior and exterior lighting and to monitor the heating and air-conditioning systems as well.

With antique brick, bay windows, and a wood-shingle roof, Watson's house looks much like every other house in the neighborhood; it's what's inside that sets his home apart. For an additional $1,900 on a $159,000 house, homeowners can have computers that greet them at the door upon arriving home and alert them if there has been an unauthorized entry. Ron Watson plans to market his product for both new and existing homes.

Fifteen hundred miles away, just outside San Diego, another high-tech home is under construction. This one was designed by two former sorority sisters and a friend who were looking for a computer that would provide home security, adjust household appliances, and monitor day-to-day activities of the family. The result:

"Home Guardian"—originally (and appropriately) named "User Friendly."

Operated by an Apple IIE, Home Guardian offers a sophisticated security system. By day, a ring of the doorbell activates video cameras which send a signal to the television. The TV turns on a designated channel so that anyone at home can view the visitor. If the visitor is unwelcome, a push of a button instructs the computer to announce, "No one is home." By night, an infrared detection system, sensitive to body heat, detects prowlers on the premises. If one is discovered, a message is sent to the computer, which lights up the house like a Christmas tree.

The system also performs such mundane chores as operating the heating and air-conditioning, opening and closing garage doors, and, through the use of thermisters—computer-controlled thermostats—operating the pump and water heater on a home aquarium.

Family appointments and schedules can be programmed up to two years ahead of time, with the computer posting reminders on the television screen on the appropriate day. When family members are at home, the system can be shut down and the computer used for homework, household accounting, or games. Waking the family, starting the coffeepot in the morning, and greeting owners as they arrive home are other tasks tirelessly performed by the Home Guardian.

Two circuit boards protect the system from losing its programs because of power outages. A custom-designed house is not a requirement, only an alcove or other out-of-the-way corner in which to mount the computer. Starting at $4,000 for the basic system and, depending on optional components, reaching $13,000 to $14,000, Trigon Computer Electronics plans to target small businesses and the retrofit of existing homes as its primary markets.

An even more ambitious project is being coordinated by the National Association of Home Builders Research Foundation in cooperation with financial institutions, manufacturers, trade associations, and government agencies. Scheduled to open in 1987, the "Smart House" will be built at a new National Research Test Park on fifty residential acres in Bowie, Maryland. Twenty-five businesses with homebuilding products are funding the project to test new types of insulation, plumbing, wiring, energy-saving devices, and totally new household products. A primary objective of the team effort is to produce a high-tech house that is easy to use by the young, the elderly, the infirm, and, of course, the technophobe.

A new wiring system will reduce or eliminate electrical shock and fire hazards while providing full flexibility for consumer control and automation of all household appliances, devices, and utilities. One single-cable wiring system with a computerized controller will bring together television cable, telephones, security, appliances, and thermostats. Within a few years, researchers expect it to be possible to telephone the Smart House and have the house cooled or heated and dinner cooking by the time occupants return home.

WHO—OR WHAT—IS MINDING THE HOUSE?

Industry observers anticipate a full-scale marriage of high-tech and down-home living over the next couple of decades. In 1986, many newly constructed homes will come equipped with computer-controlled heating, air conditioning, and security systems. Increasingly, consumers will blend technology with personal style in home furnishings for a high-tech high-touch balance.

At present, however, some caution that before committing to an enormous capital outlay, homeowners should determine whether the system being considered will do enough work around the house to justify the investment. Some insist that a "dedicated" system is more practical and less expensive than a complete system tied into a computer which, although it can be used for other things, usually can't serve two functions at once. So if the kids want to do their homework or Mom wants to balance the checkbook, the computer first has to be told to stop minding the house.

One such dedicated system is General Electric's HomeMinder. Connected to a house's existing electrical and telephone wiring, HomeMinder performs a mind-boggling array of household chores. Using the television set as the "window" of command, which makes it easy to understand, program, and monitor the device, the user presses buttons on a controller and follows pictures and instructions that are displayed on the screen. These guide the user through every step of the operation. Users can program lights or appliances to turn on today, tomorrow, every day, every weekend, every other weekend, or on specific days, with multiple on/off cycles possible during a twenty-four-hour period. An "all units" command lets users shut down or power up every attached appliance simultaneously. The system can be accessed and operated from anywhere in the country by using a Touch-Tone phone.

Available in two models, a "stand-alone" unit that can be hooked into any television set and a controller that is built into the back of a twenty-five-inch television set, HomeMinder systems sell for $500 and $1,200, respectively. A GE spokesperson, with understandable enthusiasm, asserted that within ten years, 40 to 50 percent of U.S. consumers will want the product. A recent agreement with Ryan Homes Inc. may help GE achieve its market penetration goal. Last April, Ryan Homes began providing the stand-alone unit as standard equipment in all the homes the company builds in twenty-five markets, including Texas and the East Coast.

HomeMinder is by no means the only system on the market. Hypertek Inc. makes a sophisticated, and expensive, home-control system that includes security, fire safety and lighting controls, energy management, and vacation protection in its basic package. HomeBrain's standard package costs slightly more than $2,100, plus installation charges of up to $1,500. Among other things, HomeBrain is a smoke detector. When a fire triggers an alarm, the system turns on lights to help residents find their way out of the house, flashes outside lights to signal the fire department, sets off sirens, turns off heating and ventilation systems, and triggers a phone call to the fire department.

Anova Electronics, a division of West Bend, now sells a set of tabletop components that integrates light and appliance control, telecommunication, and home protection, all for $900. BSR offers its X-10 system, a network of remote-control devices. Both Avonics and BSR models function by sending coded "phantom" signals through the home's electrical wiring network. Signal-receiving modules plugged into AC outlets react to the messages, switching any attached appliances on or off. Commands can be overridden by manually operating individual appliances.

APPLIANCES WITH A COLLEGE DEGREE

While many of us are not yet ready to live in homes with a higher intelligence quotient than our own, most of us already spend time in rooms that are a whole lot smarter than they used to be. Virtually every manufacturer of home appliances produces models equipped with microprocessors. The next generation of appliances not only will be smart, it will be multitalented, performing several different tasks at the flick of a switch. Sunbeam researchers already are hard at work developing a new line of such products.

In the year ahead, a preponderance of ordinary appliances will talk to themselves, to their owners, and to each other. Kitchens are fast evolving into "operation central," with enough high-tech hardware to make them the envy of a sci-fi filmmaker. A study conducted for Whirlpool Corp. by the University of Southern California concluded that by the year 2000, the kitchen will be obsolete. In its place will be a multipurpose planning and entertainment center, a compact and efficient setup of integrated electronic appliances and equipment.

For some time now, an appliance has been able to talk to itself, turning itself on or off and responding to preset commands to change temperature. Not long after they started talking to themselves, appliances began talking to users. "Civilized" clock radios now greet listeners with a gentle "good morning," rather than an offensive buzz. They also announce exactly how much time they will give a sleeping person before they awaken him or her again. Almost any inanimate object can be programmed to talk with a $5 computer chip. Bathroom scales can tell you how much you weigh today, how much you weighed yesterday, and how many pounds you lost since last week. (Unfortunately, they can't tell you what you'll weigh tomorrow.)

The technology exists for appliances to talk to one another. It's being done in the laboratory and soon will be available for home appliances. When a user programs an electronically controlled dishwasher to come on at a certain time, the dishwasher will communicate with the control on the water heater to provide the right temperature of water and to turn off when the cycle is complete.

As the kitchen goes, so goes the rest of the house. While not all of us are prepared to give our kitchens over to talking stovetops, microwaves, or refrigerators, most of us are dazzled by electronics designed to entertain, educate, and free us to work at home. Family rooms, bedrooms, and dens are being transformed into media centers. Two components are driving a recent surge in interest in electronic activity centers—the remarkably successful and ever more versatile videocassette recorder (VCR) and the increasingly popular home computer.

According to the Electronics Industry Association, over 7 million VCRs were sold in 1984—almost twice the 1983 figure and four times as many as in 1982. In 1985, sales approached 10 million units. Now in 17 percent of American homes, the VCR is vital to home entertainment centers because it weds conventional audio and video systems. The marriage makes possible almost a theater environment in the home. As it becomes possible to simultaneously transmit enhanced video signals to television monitors and improved audio signals to stereo speakers, movie-theater-quality entertainment will be brought into the home.

With the first wave of digital televisions just arriving from Japan, home-screen picture quality can equal that of 35mm film. Vastly improved picture quality is made possible by doubling the 525 lines on a regular set. Although more pricey than practical right now—$1,000 plus—as more sets become available, prices will drop and high-resolution TV will dramatically change home entertainment.

DIGITAL TV CREATES A WHOLE NEW PICTURE

Besides producing better quality pictures—a real boon to advertisers eager to show products in all their intricate detail—digital TVs offer a range of features that so far have been impossible or prohibitively expensive. Actually a computer and a television in the same unit, the sets use five silicon chips that replace 300,000 transistors. These chips allow two-channel viewing, zoom effects, stereo sound, and "universal" TV compatibility. Universal compatibility is not significant for American viewers, as broadcasting standards are the same across the country, but in Europe, where digital TV has been available for a while, contending with different transmission standards frequently has made television viewing a challenge. Universal compatibility will become more important to American viewers as satellite technology allows us to receive overseas signals.

More mundane features, but equally salable, include the ability to automatically compensate for some problems plaguing standard televisions. "Ghosts," for instance, will be greatly diminished. Flickering and rolling that occur when transmission is temporarily interrupted will disappear as the digital's microchip remembers the proper transmission timing and averages it out over several successive images.

Digital technology is in its infancy. More is yet to come. As its ability to memorize information improves, digital TV will become more interactive—sets will begin performing many of the functions once reserved for computers. In fact, the marriage of televisions and computers is not far off. This may be why Sony, a company associated with video and audio equipment, recently began marketing a personal computer. Noted David Kawakami of Sony's Image Display Products Division, "It's tied to the semiconductor technology. As we increase the memory, TVs become more like computers. At the same time, computers are improving their video capabilities and are becoming more like TVs."

This computer/television hybrid will become the center of an entirely new concept in home entertainment and home-based information processing. Computers, telephones, and word processors will be interconnected, making it possible to shop—via videotex—telecommute (work from a home office), bank, play, or simply be entertained without ever leaving your easy chair.

Although currently available stereo sound is good enough for amateur music lovers, audiophiles interested in high-quality sound are shifting to compact digital disk players. Manufactured by Sony and Phillips, among others, and retailing for about $500, disk players use lasers to track 4.7-inch hard disks engraved with a musical computer code. So far the machines can't record music digitally. In fact, no one is selling a consumer product that can. However, a company that went public in 1983 at 2 cents a share has a shot at this market.

Denver-based Compusonics, the brainchild of David Schwartz, a computer engineer and amateur musician, has invented a digital machine that records music on ordinary magnetic disks. Some experts insist that it offers the same clarity and fidelity as laser disk players. The company currently sells a $35,000 digital recorder to the professional market, and next year will launch a $1,200 digital recorder for the home that will make recordings on a floppy disk. Technologically, the biggest hurdle was finding a way to put a lot of music (which is data-intensive) on a magnetic disk. Compusonics does this through a kind of electronic shorthand.

Although there is some skepticism that Compusonics can win the market before the Japanese begin putting music on digital tape, the company is moving toward making its floppy disk the standard. This year, McIntosh Laboratory Inc., a manufacturer of high-quality amplifiers, will build floppy-disk recorders based on Compusonics's technology.

If the technology takes hold, the sky's the limit. Company officials are talking to AT&T about setting up a service that would enable record companies to sell directly to consumers over the telephone. Jazz concerts, ordered by credit card, could travel digitally over phone lines into homes to be recorded by Compusonics's machine. Movies also could be recorded digitally and sent the same way. The year 1986 could well see the birth of a whole new market. Speculators have shown enough interest to drive Compusonics's stock up 525 percent in two years, to almost 13 cents a share.

HIGH-TOUCH FURNISHINGS FOR HIGH-TECH ENVIRONMENT

High-tech appliances, media centers, and computer-controlled personal environments are forcing the home furnishings industry to take a careful look at where it is and to decide how it should position itself in the future. As interested as consumers are in state-of-the-art products, they still want their homes to look like homes and to be comfortable places to live. Technology may change what goes on inside, but comfort, design, and attractiveness will remain the standard for furnishings. Many in the industry already have responded to consumer demands for attractively designed, color-coordinated entertainment units and accompanying furnishings. While some audio-video equipment manufacturers offer serviceable units, virtually every cabinet or furniture maker now offers home entertainment units. In the year ahead, this market will explode.

If electronic homes are already here, can electronic villages be far behind? Don Power and Josh Wilson, managing partners of a development in Foresthill, California, are counting on it. Eaglecrest is a "fledgling, computer-oriented housing development" which its developers believe is a prototype of the electronic village of the future. Eaglecrest's first model, built with the electronic commuter in mind, features an intricate wire network of twelve pairs of lines for telephone, data, and coaxial cable. The network enables the home to function as an electronic center for "domestic administration, entertainment, education, and occupational activities." Each home in the development will be equipped with a computer that can be linked to the owner's office, providing both voice and data access simultaneously.

Eaglecrest has received critical acclaim for its integration of architectural styling, energy efficiency, and state-of-the-art computer circuitry. But it's too early to judge whether there is a market for isolated electronic villages, where home and office are contained in one unit. Considering that many of us go to the office as much for the social stimulation as to get work done, it's hard to imagine many people giving that up. (Of course, some of us might choose to work at home during emergencies—like Mondays and Fridays.)

OFFICE BUILDINGS AND EXECUTIVE SUITES IMPROVE THEIR IQ

Technology-enhanced real estate—smart buildings—is the latest buzzword among commercial realtors. Soon it may translate into big bucks for builders, realtors, and manufacturers of integrated electronic systems, the systems that give buildings their brains.

McLean, Virginia–based Planning Research Corp. (PRC), an international engineering and information services company, provides its building tenants with shared telecommunications services using a computerized device manufactured by Northern Telecom Inc. Called a PBX (private branch exchange), the device is a high-tech descendant of the once-familiar office switchboard, with one dramatic difference—the PBX is capable of transmitting voice and data simultaneously.

The PBX makes it possible for tenants to share telephone lines and services, to tie personal computers into prewired networks, and to centralize electronic message delivery. In PRC's building, tenants' long-distance calls are automatically routed through the least expensive lines over a shared telecommunications network. Costs for local calls are cut by sharing local telephone company lines. Calls can be forwarded to a centralized message center when tenants are not in their offices, and general office tasks such as telexing, telecopying, and sending cablegrams can all be channeled through the electronic mail center.

PRC's building is smart, but there are others even smarter. Buildings elsewhere offer everything PRC does, as well as elevators that announce floors and give directions, and infrared detectors that "see" if there are people in a room and turn the lights on or off accordingly. A network of sensors and computers controls the temperature, security, and elevators. With mainframe computers for brains and fiber-optics cables woven throughout the building and in some cases from building to building, the systems run within strict operational parameters, monitor themselves, diagnose their own problems, and are frequently able to solve those problems without help from a human operator.

Definitions of what makes a building smart vary, but there are three basic intelligence levels. At the simplest level are computer-controlled building services: heating and air-conditioning, security, and electrical systems. The second level up includes shared telecommunications systems such as that offered by PRC. Most sophisticated of all are systems which encompass all of these as well as interconnecting data communications networks between offices and the outside world and special features like teleconferencing. By the strict standards of MCC Powers, a division of Mark Controls Corp. and a vendor of intelligent-building systems, there are only twelve truly intelligent buildings in the United States so far. But hundreds more offer the simplest level of service, and hundreds under construction eventually will offer all three levels.

DALLAS, WASHINGTON LEAD IN SHARED-TENANT BUILDINGS

Dallas is the acknowledged mecca for shared-tenant services, with Washington, D.C., running a close second. Telestrategies Inc., a McLean, Virginia–based consulting firm, estimates that buildings offering shared telecommunications systems will mushroom from the seventy already standing to 15,000 by 1994. Revenue from equipment sales and operations will climb from about $252 million to more than $12 billion as many more buildings are retrofitted to provide shared services. This will be particularly true in soft markets—cities where commercial real estate has been overbuilt and realtors need a competitive edge to survive the market.

Structures once found only at World's Fair pavilions or fantasy science parks like EPCOT Center now stand in a number of American cities. Tower Forty-Nine in New York, City Place in Hartford, LTV Center and Lincoln Plaza in Dallas, Tabor Center in Denver, and Citicorp Center in San Francisco are towering testimonials to architectural ingenuity in merging technology with individual comfort and design. All of these buildings were planned, designed, equipped, and furnished to make the people who work in them more comfortable and more productive.

Arguably, high-tech giant United Technologies Corp. (UTC) spearheaded the integration of technologies that gave birth to the intelligent building. If UTC was not alone in developing the technology, it certainly helped pave the way. UTC's patented fiber-optic data highway, called TECHLOOP, led the Hartford-based company to pioneer its application in the design of commercial office buildings. Having acquired a stable of building service companies, including Otis Elevator, Carrier (air conditioners), Hamilton Standard (makers of controls and energy management systems), and Lexar (telephone equipment), UTC formed a new subsidiary, Building Systems Co. (BSC), in 1981.

Since then, BSC has revolutionized the multitenant office building. The firm supplies building equipment and control systems along with an innovative package of tenant services offered via a partnership with AT&T Information Systems. ShareTech, as the joint venture product is called, provides shared telecommunications and information management services to developers, managers, and tenants of commercial office buildings. Scores of vendors, including many of AT&T's offspring, now sell communications hardware and communications systems. So many, in fact, that for the unschooled it is difficult to separate fact from fiction and bits from bytes or to know for sure which system best suits their needs. ShareTech was an obvious solution.

Not surprisingly, a host of other makers of building control systems and data communications manufacturers are teaming up to offer developers package deals. Honeywell is launching a joint venture with L. M. Ericsson. Their first project will be the 600,000-square-foot Renaissance Park near Washington, D.C.'s Dulles Airport. Intelligence for One Financial Plaza in Chicago will be provided by Milwaukee-based Johnson Controls, inventor of the electric thermostat back in the 1880s, and InteCom, a Texas maker of PBXs. And Mark Controls's MCC Powers division has made a similar arrangement with TeleCom to install an integrated package in Atlanta's Concourse Corporate Center.

Still others hope to win a share of the market by unbundling services. Major players include General Electric, United Telecommunications, and Northern Telecom, all of whom will attempt to convince developers that what they lack in controls technology they can more than make up for in data communications know-how. Some developers are starting their own subsidiary companies to build and service intelligent-building systems.

COST OF MAKING A BUILDING SMART—ABOUT 4 PERCENT

Competition for smart-building contracts is heating up. In the year ahead, it will become even more fierce. Revenues from a shared-tenant telephone system are about $2 million a year for a typical twenty-story, 600,000-square-foot office complex. Cost savings for both tenant and builder are enormous. The addition of intelligence to a $100-million building, at the design stage, adds only about 4 percent to the cost of the building, and returns are realized within two years. Wiring for electronic office equipment alone can be as high as $50,000 a floor in conventional buildings; that cost is eliminated in an intelligent building because of built-in data highways.

Computer controls also help reduce operating costs for such devices as climate control and lighting control systems. Sensors, which react to both outdoor and indoor temperatures, heat-generating equipment, and occupants, can reduce heating and air-conditioning costs by about 20 percent. Electricity costs for lighting can be slashed by almost 40 percent simply by having the system turn off lights in vacant offices.

Smart buildings are not without their critics. One skeptic noted that "an intelligent building is one that costs less to build and rents out quickly." Others view them as a "big hype" generated by the controls and communications industries anxious to profit from the lucrative tenant-services business. More, however, seem to share the sentiments of Allen Waller, partner in Tishman Speyer Properties of New York, one of the nation's ten largest real estate developers. Says Waller: "It makes no sense at all not to provide tenants with computer-controlled environments and telecommunications capabilities."

Even developers who hesitate to jump feet-first into the market are designing structures that can be upgraded at some future point. Design flexibility includes improved air-conditioning capabilities, increased floor loads, higher ceilings on the first floor to accommodate a PBX, and central risers that easily could be wired with fiber-optics or other connecting cables. Some developers hold back because the market is new and there are so many players; they're waiting to see which companies survive and which products earn the best track record.

SCRAMBLE TO CONTROL OFFICE AUTOMATION

Excitement over the construction of smart buildings points to another battle brewing: competition for control of the office automation market. In the eye of the storm are two pieces of standard office equipment—the telephone and the computer. During the past year, they were welded together as a host of industry giants and entrepreneurial upstarts introduced single-unit desktop machines that functioned as both. In 1986, these same players will scramble to capture contracts to link all those office units together. Local area networks (LANs) are a component of the office automation market that is strong and getting stronger. LANs, essentially, are sophisticated cabling systems that allow desktop units and workstations to "talk" to each other and to larger computers.

To date, companies have purchased most office equipment piecemeal and often from different vendors, and just as often bought several different manufacturers' products. Frequently, people in the same office were unable to share software or communicate with one another via their terminals because they were not compatible. LANs solve a host of interoffice communications problems.

LANs have been around since Datapoint Corp. introduced them in the mid-1970s, but they have not taken off for at least two reasons. One, because of industry infighting over which technology was best, and two, because IBM had not yet introduced a network. Many would-be users waited for IBM to set the standard and, by its presence in the market, endorse the very concept of an LAN. The long-awaited entry should occur soon.

Meanwhile, the industry has begun to agree on standards. A committee of the Institute of Electrical & Electronics Engineers (IEEE), made up of industry representatives, has endorsed three network schemes. Two use a technique called token passing, which links computer gear together in either a ring or a line. IBM's entry is likely to use a token ring design. A third scheme employs a collision detection/avoidance approach pioneered by Xerox Corp.'s Ethenet network. This scheme is backed by more than 100 companies that make products to work with it. AT&T is expected to go it alone, offering a design not endorsed by the IEEE.

Confusion will continue to reign. There are three distinct LAN markets. The biggest is for high-speed links between mainframe computers. Second is the market for medium-speed networks that link the various pieces of office equipment together. And the third, possibly the fastest-growing market, is for lower-speed networks that connect stand-alone personal computers to each other. Furthermore, each market segment is served both by computer manufacturers, which generally offer proprietary networks that link only their machines, and by independent network makers, specialists in LANs that work with a variety of equipment.

LOCAL AREA NETWORKS TO GROW INTO $1-BILLION INDUSTRY

Regardless of who captures which part of what market, there are dollars to be made. An analyst at Dataquest estimates that sales of LANs will top the $1-billion mark by 1988. Installation and software costs will net another $300 million a year.

LANs also serve to break down communications barriers in automated factories where it is essential that all the high-tech hardware work together. Now that standards have been set, a dramatic change on the factory floor is anticipated. Factories may well account for one-third of the $1 billion in sales of local area networks.

As technology-based products become more user friendly, and users become more comfortable with the idea that technology can, and should, serve to make work and play a little easier, the demand for smart products, smart homes, and smart offices will grow. In the year ahead, expect to see growing demand for, greater availability of, and sharply reduced prices for a dizzying array of computer-controlled systems for home and office.

Smart homes... smart offices... smart factories. If all this makes you feel as if you've been left behind in a time warp, fear not. If you have a Touch-Tone phone, you already own a computer terminal—albeit a rudimentary one. If you own a VCR and a stereo, you have the foundation of a sophisticated entertainment center.

6 RETAILING GETS A WHOLESALE FACE-LIFT. INNOVATORS GIVE TRADITIONALISTS THE BUSINESS.

By the end of 1986, thousands of fast-food aficionados will have it their way, courtesy of a six-armed robot. Programmed to do virtually anything restaurant workers can do—except maybe put its thumb in the soup—the robot will prepare meals to order, serve them, take money and make change, sweep the floor, and clear tables. Its creator, Peter Hughes, president of Hughes International (with offices in Hunt Valley, Maryland, and London), won't divulge which restaurants plan to employ his robot. But he acknowledges that four full-time designers will spend two to three months perfecting the technology to create his electronic chef. A major burger chain plans to buy at least one robot, and a national pizza chain also is interested, he says.

Wearing the restaurant's uniform and a smile, the robot will scurry around on a U-shaped track with its six-foot-long independently functioning arms reaching out in all directions—a marvel of efficiency. Its computerized "brain" will detect overcooked hamburgers (and throw them away), scan floors and countertops for spills (and wipe them up), and take instructions from customers in the order in which they sit on chairs equipped with electronic sensors. Not only will the robot's voice-activated eyes look at customers when they're ordering, but if an order takes more than fifteen seconds to arrive, the robot will sing. (That's entertainment?)

With a $100,000 price tag, the robot doesn't work cheap. It does, however, have a seven-year life span (in use twenty-four hours a day) and will tirelessly perform tasks human employees might find distasteful.

Such devices will look more and more attractive to restaurant owners over the next few years, as current labor shortages become even more severe. The number of workers in their teen years—the pool from which most fast-food restaurants draw—is dropping sharply. While not every fast-food shop will replace workers with robots, the devices could help solve severe personnel shortages.

Most business owners probably are not ready for robots, but the age of electronic retailing is nonetheless dawning and may well revolutionize the retail industry. The proliferation of home computers and the more widespread availability of videotex services will propel this infant industry to new heights. Electronic retailing is expected to skyrocket from $285 million in sales in 1985 to $17 billion by 1990, according to estimates by Chicago-based R. R. Donnelly & Sons Co., the country's largest commercial printing firm and developer of electronic in-store kiosks.

Analysts at Touche Ross & Co., one of the nation's largest retail consulting services, project more modest but nonetheless explosive growth. They estimate that by 1989 consumers will be buying between $5 billion and $10 billion of merchandise a year from 50,000 electronic in-store kiosks throughout the United States and that an additional 50,000 terminals in retail stores and other public facilities such as shopping malls will provide up-to-date information on products sold nearby. Said Thomas Ruah, a management consulting partner at Touche Ross and author of its electronic-shopping study, "Electronic shopping isn't likely to account for more than 10 percent of all general retail sales at most. But in today's dollars, that's easily $100 billion." That's no small change.

SHOPPING BY TV OR COMPUTER SCREEN

Just what is electronic shopping? That's difficult to define. It exists in a variety of forms, with varying degrees of sophistication. Consumers can shop electronically from the comfort of their living room via videotex displayed on a television screen or home computer. In shopping malls and other retail outlets, they may find in-store kiosks equipped with electronic informational directories or computer software programs that allow them to browse through merchandise directories, select an item, and pay with a credit card, all on the same terminal.

Stamford, Connecticut–based Comp-U-Card International Inc. and R. R. Donnelly are two companies on the cutting edge of electronic shopping. Their products are representative of what is available in at-home and in-store technology.

According to Comp-U-Card chairman Walter A. Forbes, "Comp-U-Card was founded upon the idea that the next major revolution in retailing would offer the consumer the choice of shopping electronically from the convenience of home." He may be onto something. Some 1.5 million members (up from 450,000 in 1983)—with more to come from licensed operations in twenty-nine markets worldwide, including Canada, Japan, and England—have access to 60,000 brand-name products. The products come with full manufacturers' warranties, at savings of up to 50 percent over in-store prices, and they're all available via home computers.

Comp-U-Card's 170 employees also are busy developing the Electronic Mall, which will offer such merchandise as gourmet foods, flowers, paintings, books, apparel, auto supplies, and computers. The Electronic Mall will be available to customers who enroll in the company's On Line program, enabling them to order directly from such retailers as Neiman-Marcus, Saks Fifth Avenue, and I. Magnin.

R. R. Donnelly's Electronistore offers electronic shopping via a different route. Electronistore allows retailers to expand their product lines without adding expensive floor space or even salespeople. Located in a freestanding kiosk resembling a video arcade, the Electronistore has a nineteen-inch color monitor for product display, product information, and order placement. Audio presentations are made possible through a stereo sound system within the kiosk. Orders can be placed with a credit card—retailers decide which cards will be accepted. An internal printer prepares receipts.

What sets Electronistore apart from other freestanding units, according to its developer, is that it's the first system that lets retailers change the electronic display of products daily.

Comp-U-Card and Donnelly are joined by others in an area of retailing that is just beginning to gain momentum. Among them are CompuServe in Columbus, Ohio, a subsidiary of H&R Block Inc.; CompuSave in Los Angeles, which is essentially another Comp-U-Card; ByVideo, developer of Uniport, a system similar to Electronistore; and various retailers' own in-house systems.

MAKING A GAME OUT OF SHOPPING

Also called transactional systems, electronic shopping outlets are showing up in all sorts of places, selling all kinds of merchandise. Often the devices are designed to keep up with changing life-style and work habits. These days, when the Avon lady comes calling, as often as not there is no one home. Avon Products Inc. overcame that obstacle by installing eight Uniports in malls and office concourses in Hartford, Connecticut, and eight more in similar locations in Raleigh, North Carolina. Said Joanne Jaeger, spokeswoman for the company, "It's a way of reaching hard-to-reach customers, primarily working women. So far, they seem very positive. People like to play with them. It's like a video game."

Florsheim Shoe Co. of Chicago has installed freestanding kiosks in malls where it does not have stores—in Bloomington, Indiana, Ames, Iowa, Glendale, Wisconsin, and Port Arthur, Texas. The machines offer 250 styles of men's shoes. To the question of whether a customer really will buy shoes from a machine, a representative of ByVideo noted, "It's the kind of shoe company where you've been buying shoes there for years and you know your size. You can buy any color, any size that Florsheim makes, while typically a store can't carry all that."

And that's the point. Electronic shopping is an option, for both retailers and consumers. Because they can be set up anywhere—currently, they are being placed in shopping malls, but soon will be in supermarkets, health spas, and hotel lobbies—electronic-shopping outlets represent an added convenience for consumers and low overhead for business.

This is true for videotex services as well, but so far they haven't enjoyed the growth rates anticipated when they were originally conceived. Generically, videotex (sometimes called videotext) is any information service that lets the public get data from, and send messages to, a central computer. (Technically, Electronistore is a videotex system, but videotex is more commonly used to describe systems accessed from home or office.) Some videotex services are designed for use with personal computers; others require a special box attached to a television set.

To date, videotex services that are primarily informational but also offer shopping services—such as CompuServe, with 200,000 subscribers, and the Source, owned by Reader's Digest Association Inc., with 63,000 subscribers—are doing reasonably well. However, services aimed exclusively at the home-shopping market are struggling. Knight-Ridder's Viewtron; Keyfax, which is a joint venture between Chicago-based Centel Corp. and Honeywell Inc.; and Gateway, a Times Mirror Co. service, all have far fewer subscribers than they'd hoped to attract. Industry observers blame this on a slower than projected penetration of personal computers in homes and on high on-line telephone service charges.

Initial difficulties have not quelled interest in videotex. IBM, CBS Inc., and Sears, Roebuck & Co. are developing a service called Trintex, aimed at the home computer market. Other major players include RCA Corp. in a joint venture with Citicorp, and AT&T in partnership with Chemical Bank, Bank of America, and Time Inc. All believe they can improve service by upgrading systems, taking advantage of lower cost AT&T long-line competitors, and improving content. Some also count on increased usage as more people gain access to personal computers both in the office and at home.

Notwithstanding such optimism, all of the principles involved in videotex ventures are realistic. None of these companies expects electronic shopping to replace in-store shopping, but they believe they offer a valuable option. Says Harry Smith, vice-president for videotex publishing at Trintex, "Videotex has the potential to save people time and money and do a lot of things that people will find enjoyable and life-enhancing." Maybe. But most of us will never give up the serendipity of shopping. Touching, feeling, trying on, and trying out are all part of the fun. Electronic shopping will serve us well only for articles or products for which we already have established standards of quality and price range. For everything else there is no substitute for the real thing.

SHOPPING WITH A ROBOT AT YOUR SIDE

Currently, the ultimate in-store electronic-shopping experience can be found only in Japan. Seibu Department Stores has packed every imaginable modern gadget into its experimental Department Store of the Future in Tsukuba, near Tokyo. With the help of some of Japan's giant electronic and computer companies, Seibu has created a high-tech wonderland. Robots follow shoppers everywhere, carrying packages and making themselves generally useful. If the shopper stops, the robot stops. If the shopper turns, the robot turns.

In-store computers list every available product in the store and where to find it. The computers also help with clothing selections, suggest fabric, and keep records of a customer's size and build. Looking for sportswear? Thanks to laser-disk background screens, sports buffs can try on apparel against the appropriate background —tennis courts, golf greens, or whatever. Kids can be left in a baby-sitting room and kept tabs on via television phones. And when a customer is all shopped out, the robot carries the purchases to a waiting attendant who whisks the shopper and packages, aboard an electronic cart, back to the parking lot.

RETAILERS FACE A MASSIVE SHAKEOUT

The retail industry is in tumult. Many outlets will fold or be gobbled up by bigger stores before the end of 1986. Department stores are battling off-price retailers for market share. Manufacturers and mail-order houses are opening retail outlets. Sears, K mart, and J. C. Penney want to be everything to everybody. And merger mania has infected many in the industry.

Some chains are booming. In eight years, Dress Barn Inc. has blossomed from 18 stores clustered on the East Coast to 157 stores nationwide. Sales during 1985 are expected to increase 55 percent over 1984 receipts, to $95 million, and the company plans to add 150 stores by 1990. Clearly, the firm is doing something right.

Dress Barn is doing what thousands of others are doing: buying late-in-the-season fashions, buying in bulk, and slashing prices on designer and brand-name clothing and shoes. The company is representative of the explosive growth in off-price retailing, which has grown from 1,000 such stores in 1971 to 10,000 in 1984, with sales of $8.5 billion. Adhering to the philosophy that if one is good, more are better, entire malls devoted to off-price shopping now dot the country. In 1981, there were fifty-four; by mid-1985, the number exceeded 300.

Not surprisingly, a shakeout is already under way. An analyst with Johnson Redbook Service lists the following off-pricers as experiencing some degree of difficulty: Syms Corp., Burlington Coat Factory, Marshalls Inc. (a division of Melville Corp.), Loehmann's (a division of Associated Dry Goods Inc.), J. Brennam (owned by F. W. Woolworth), and T. H. Mandy (owned by U.S. Shoe Corp.). Things are likely to get worse before they get better.

Stronger firms are poised to acquire weaker chains, a pattern that analysts expect to continue through 1987. Among Dress Barn's recent purchases are Off-the-Rax, a forty-eight-store chain owned by Stop & Shop Cos., and eight Tagg stores, owned by The Gap Stores Inc. In time there will be fewer off-pricers, but survivors are expected to increase their share of the retail clothing market to 13 percent by 1990, with sales of close to $25 billion annually.

Successful off-pricers also are giving themselves a face-lift, making their stores more appealing. They feature attractive display areas and private dressing rooms, offer return policies, and accept credit cards. Why, when they already had a winning formula? Because their market niche is saturated and because department stores have begun to compete with them on their own turf.

After a decade during which department stores enjoyed a high degree of pricing flexibility, off-price retailers presented more traditional retailers with a very real challenge—to meet them in pricing and beat them with service and selection. Many traditional retailers rose to the challenge by slashing prices. Said Isaac Lagnado, director of research for Associated Merchandising Corp., a New York City retail consulting firm: "Ten years ago, department stores did 30 percent of their business at markdown. Five years ago, that had risen to 50 percent. Recently, though, nearly 75 percent of their business is markdown." Other retailers advertised quality, selection, and service advantages. Needless to say, promotions and price-cutting pared profit margins and market shares of many established merchants.

MORE STORES VS. LESS DISPOSABLE INCOME

The industry will be even more volatile in the year ahead. An overwhelming similarity in merchandise available at either department stores or off-price retailers has encouraged consumers to use price as the primary differentiating factor. Moreover, an increasing reliance by retailers on price promotions as the primary means to stimulate store traffic has conditioned consumers to wait for sales and clearance markdowns on seasonal goods. Furthermore, some industry analysts insist that America is "overstored" and that high housing, utility, and medical costs leave consumers with less disposable income to spend on general merchandise. All of this puts even more pressure on retailers.

According to *Shopping Center World*, a trade publication that makes a biennial survey of shopping centers, the number of shopping centers rose 70 percent and square footage increased 80 percent from 1974 to 1984. However, the population expanded by only 12 percent, so the shopping center space per capita went from 7.7 to 14 square feet over the decade. To sustain profits, American retailers gradually pushed markups to 90 or 100 percent, seeking gross profits of 45 to 50 percent. Discounters tagged markups of 60 percent and margins of 30 percent. Price wars changed all that. Many retailers are in trouble.

American retailing practices baffle their European and Japanese counterparts. They find the poor productivity of U.S. stores, as measured in sales per square foot, hard to understand. They don't see how American retailers can make a profit, much less continue to add stores, when their annual sales per square foot average $130, about one-third of European stores.

Some American analysts also find the situation baffling and warn of a major industry upheaval. Cognizant of the dangers ahead, many retailers are designing new survival strategies. For industry powerhouses such as R. H. Macy & Co., Dayton-Hudson Corp., The Limited Inc., and Federated Department Stores Inc., strategies include penetrating new markets (even saturated markets, counting on name recognition and a reputation for quality and affordability to keep them afloat), identifying and serving specialized market niches, and buying out or merging with weaker links.

Minneapolis-based Dayton-Hudson Corp. has allocated $3.2 billion for expansion of its retail operations over the next five years. Eighty percent of that will be invested in its Mervyn's and Target department store chains. Already, Mervyn's has successfully penetrated the overdeveloped Houston market, and did so even as Macy's and a raft of off-price retailers such as Ross Stores, Designer Depot, and Siegels were in the midst of a building frenzy in that area. Despite stiff competition, 1984 sales in Mervyn's Texas stores were $260 million, about 10 percent above projections.

Federated Department Stores Inc., on the other hand, decided to introduce a new chain. The Cincinnati-based department store chain opened three MainStreet stores in Chicago in 1984 and six more in 1985, and will open at least as many in 1986. Federated plans to take the chain national but has not identified its other projected markets.

MainStreet signals a new approach for Federated, the nation's largest department store operator. Traditionally, it has preferred to buy successful regional concerns or spin off departments of existing stores, rather than build retail chains from scratch. MainStreet is intended to fill the gap between bare-bones discounters and department stores. Targeted at middle-income consumers, the stores will offer more than 70 percent of their merchandise in national brand names. They are also pitching better customer service, promising about one-third more salespeople per square foot than traditional department stores and greater access to cash registers. No lines, they hope.

FLURRY OF MERGERS, ACQUISITIONS AHEAD

Mergers are becoming increasingly attractive to some retailers. When Ames Department Stores and G. C. Murphy announced that Ames would acquire Murphy, Ames's common stock shot up. In fact, both stocks rose. That's surprising, considering that an acquiring company's stock generally falls while the acquired company's stock rises. That acquisition, and another in which Zayre Corp. increased its stake in the Gaylords National Corp. in preparation for a tender offer, are the latest takeover moves in this tumultuous industry.

More mergers can be expected. Large diversified retailers are on a growth pattern that all but forces them to acquire specialized businesses. The ever-rising cost of real estate and the slowdown in shopping center construction have raised the value of smaller companies in the eyes of major players. A flurry of horizontal mergers and acquisitions—retailers buying retailers—will characterize this market in 1986. At the same time, boutiques will continue to attract shoppers. These entrepreneurial units emphasize service, style, and quality tailored to specific market niches.

On the other hand, being all things to all people is a strategy available to only a handful. Sears, Roebuck & Co., J. C. Penney, and K mart are among them. All three have diversified and flourished. They are retailers, bankers, insurance carriers, automotive shops, and home-repair centers. They are everywhere and they have a loyal following. Now they're upgrading their stores—growing up with the baby boomers, whose parents they served for years.

On a less sweeping level, bookstores are diversifying their product lines to reach a broad section of baby boomers—commuters, working mothers, and executives. Capitalizing on the popularity of the Sony Walkman, large book chains offer novels, plays, children's stories, and business-oriented books on tape. Waldenbooks has its own Waldentapes line. B. Dalton sells children's cassette-book combinations and may add an adult line. Seeking to become an all-purpose infostore, rather than merely a bookstore, Crown Book Corp., a discount chain, announced plans to sell video and audio tapes. The decision to sell tapes comes a year after Crown began selling computer software in 50 of its 181 stores. Sales of audioliterary cassettes are up 100 percent since 1981.

Meanwhile, there are some exciting new market entries as manufacturers and mail-order retailers cross over and European retailers look for a home away from home.

Taking a cue from fashion designers such as Yves Saint Laurent and Giorgio Armani, apparel manufacturers are opening their own retail outlets, convinced they can show department stores a thing or two about displaying garments and building sales. After experimenting with the concept in Hong Kong, Esprit de Corp—manufacturer of medium-priced, mix-and-match casual clothing—has opened a 30,000-square-foot emporium in Los Angeles. Plowing more than $10 million into its first U.S. venture, this San Francisco–based company is convinced that the right ambience and a relaxed, soft-sell approach will dramatically increase its profits—already $800 million a year internationally.

Esprit is not alone. Murjani International is opening two stores in 1985, featuring a new line of clothes with (of all things) the Coca-Cola label, and chairman Mohan B. Murjani talks about having hundreds more stores. Eileen West of San Francisco and sportswear manufacturers Guess? and Cherokee, both of Los Angeles, are jumping on the bandwagon. The various manufacturers insist that these moves are defensive measures. Department stores, they say, have come to rely on big names such as Calvin Klein and Liz Claiborne or on private labels to earn the most revenue per square foot. That hurts small manufacturers. In addition, sales staff reductions mean there are no people on the department store floor to chat with customers about new lines. Consequently, consumers don't discover what lesser-known manufacturers have to offer.

Mail-order retailers also are taking the plunge. They're crossing over to earn the respect—and business—of consumers who would rather feel it, touch it, and try it on before buying. In seven years, Royal Silk Ltd. has grown from a start-up mail-order firm to its current position as the reigning silk vendor of the catalog crowd. In 1984, the company sold $22 million worth of Asian-made clothing and accessories to more than 400,000 customers. That's good, but how about the millions who got away? To attract those, Royal Silk opened its first store two years ago, near its headquarters in Clifton, New Jersey. Since then stores have opened in Greensboro, North Carolina, and Freeport, Maine. By the end of 1985, three more will have opened. Currently, store sales account for less than 5 percent of the company's annual revenues, but they're expected to reach 20 percent during the next five years.

Other mail-order retailers who have decided to become more visible include Victoria's Secret, a lingerie company owned by The Limited Inc., of Columbus, Ohio, with twenty stores currently and twenty-nine more scheduled to open; San Francisco–based The Sharper Image, which sells "toys for the corporate executive," opened its first full-service store in 1980 and now has outlets in Denver, Los Angeles, and Houston; and Banana Republic Travel & Safari Clothing Co., a catalog and retail operation that specializes in surplus military and safari-style clothing, which grew from one store to eleven stores in just three years. Although clustered on the West Coast, Banana Republic also has opened stores in Washington, D.C., Houston, New York, and Chicago.

All agree that their primary motivation in opening retail outlets was to legitimize their catalog operations. Their aim is to convert retail outlet customers to the mail-order mentality, a logical crossover. Meanwhile, some companies that are primarily outlet retailers are moving into the catalog business as well. Eventually, there will be hundreds of hybrids.

EUROPEAN RETAILERS STEP UP THEIR U.S. INVOLVEMENT

Competition, price slashing, too many stores, and too few customers have done little to dissuade European retailers from moving into American markets. Bumping up against limits to growth in their home markets, Europeans are hungry for new outlets. Continued strength of the dollar also is a powerful incentive. By using distinctive retailing approaches, carefully targeting their audience, and controlling the design and manufacture of their merchandise, European retailers expect to succeed where many American retailers fail.

An Italian clothing manufacturer named Benetton has made a big splash on New York's Fifth Avenue. Employing a strategy that served it well at home, Benetton adapts each store to the neighborhood in which it opens. And it is everywhere at once—sometimes stores open across the street from one another. Benetton is aggressive. Starting with five U.S. shops in 1979, it has opened 200 since and expects to launch another 200 by the close of 1985.

A Swedish furniture retailer, IKEA, also has grand plans for the U.S. market. IKEA opened a three-acre store in the Philadelphia suburb of Plymouth, selling home furnishings at prices at least 20 percent less than the competition. According to an IKEA officer, prices are held down by manufacturing in large production runs and by cutting service costs. For example, customers select their merchandise with few salespeople present, get it from the warehouse themselves, and assemble it at home.

Another concept introduced by overseas competitors is one familiar to French consumers: *hypermarché*, or hypermarket in English. French retailer Euromarche last fall built the first hypermarket in Cincinnati. It's called Bigg's, and it is. The operation includes an oversize supermarket and a huge department store under a single roof.

Not all foreign operations immediately take the country by storm. Many have to adjust to American peculiarities. Laura Ashley Ltd. discovered that America's fashion seasons are longer than those in Europe and that the Europeans' successful strategy of opening shops in off-the-beaten-track locations failed in places like San Francisco—Americans simply don't bother to look for them. Ashley now opens most of its stores in malls or on Main Street. Benetton's also had some adjustments to make. European shoppers prefer intimate boutique settings. American shoppers expect room to move around in. In Europe, Benetton's stores are no more than 600 to 700 square feet; in this country, they're 800 to 1,000 square feet.

Small difficulties aside, European retailers see the American market as almost limitless and a first-rate opportunity for growth. Increasingly, retail outlets will carry names with a foreign accent.

MARKETING TO YUPPIES—AND ALL THE REST

The year ahead promises to be an exciting and challenging one for retailers. Competition will be stiffer than it has ever been. Consumers are better educated and more demanding, and they've grown accustomed to quality products at affordable prices. Although recent reports suggest that the most remarkable thing about the current generation of shoppers—the ubiquitous baby boomers—is their totally unremarkable spending habits, there is money to be made if only because there are more of them.

Baby boomers are in their prime spending years. All have entered the work force; many have started families. They may not spend more than their parents do on general merchandise, but there are more of them spending it. This much-discussed generation seems to fall into two categories—Yuppies and all the rest.

Yuppies, who for the most part belong to the older third of this giant generation, spend on quality. Service is important and so, apparently, is status. They have fewer children than their parents did, they are better educated (they are also better educated than their younger siblings), and they have had greater job opportunities. Upscale is a word associated with Yuppies. For them, price is less important than quality.

The rest—the other two-thirds of the bulge—also demand quality, but price competitiveness is essential. Frequently, they're part of a two-income family, by necessity. Current housing prices being what they are, this group couldn't afford a home in most areas if both partners didn't work. Quality counts, but price is almost always the determining factor. Selling to this group requires retailers to offer convenient location, good prices, and reasonable quality.

In 1986, the retailer who is able to identify a market niche and to meet consumer expectations in that niche will fare well. Retailers who try to be all things to all people, or who miss a key component, will be washed away in a tidal wave of competition.

7 LASER TECHNOLOGY TRANSFORMS INDUSTRY. WE'RE ALL BEGINNING TO SEE THE LIGHT.

On May 15, 1960, the most intensely pure beam of light the world had ever seen flashed out of a solid ruby crystal. The laser was born. Invented by Dr. Theodore H. Maiman at Hughes Research Laboratories in Malibu, California, the laser evolved in twenty-five years from little more than an exotic flashlight into an indispensable tool in medicine, industry, electronics, data processing, communications, and scientific research. According to *Lasers & Applications* magazine, more than a million lasers were sold for medical and industrial use in North America, Western Europe, and Japan in 1984—twice as many as in 1983—for a total of $416 million in sales.

When military applications are calculated, this onetime laboratory curiosity now represents a billion-dollar industry. Military laser equipment and services will reach $4.25 billion in sales by 1988, up from $2.06 billion in fiscal 1983, according to one market research firm.

Medical lasers are used for removing birthmarks, for removing plaque from clogged arteries, and for heart surgery. New applications are discovered yearly. By the close of 1985, sales of medical laser systems will have grown from a $181-million industry to $330 million. Laser technology used in the transmission of voice and data already is a multimillion-dollar industry.

Assigning a dollar value to lasers used in other industries is more difficult. Suffice it to say that collectively the development and application of laser technology for industrial uses, for education and training, and for entertainment also is a multimillion-dollar-a-year industry. In factories, supermarkets, and production lines, lasers scan bar codes for inventory, sales, and record keeping. Police crime labs use lasers to detect fingerprints. The computer industry uses them to make optical disk drives for dense computer storage. The entertainment industry relies on lasers to produce high-quality audiodisks. Data communications is greatly enhanced by laser printers and fiber-optics cables, now used around the world in state-of-the-art communications networks.

What is this miraculous technology? The word "laser" is an acronym for "light amplified by stimulated emission of radiation." The lasing effect is achieved when atoms, which exist at low and high energy levels, are excited to greater levels of activity, usually by heating but also by being bombarded by light of a higher frequency. On reaching higher levels and then returning to lower levels, atoms give off light.

Atoms in any substance—gases, liquids, organic dyes, rare-earth elements (rubies and sapphires, for example), and certain chemical compounds are among the substances used in laser technology—emit light independently and in many different colors, or wavelengths. During the brief time an atom is excited, if light of a certain color impinges on it, the atom can be stimulated to emit radiation. The radiation amplifies the light. If the phenomenon is multiplied sufficiently—that is, if all the atoms are excited to the same level of energy—the resulting beam, made up of wholly coherent light of a single color, will be extremely powerful.

Laser light can be directed, or focused, with conventional lens systems to a specific spot. Because laser light is so intense, it can burn through almost anything. Ruby lasers, for example, are used to drill holes in diamonds for wire-carrying dies and in sapphires for watch bearings. Heating effects produced by a pulsed laser beam (a beam interrupted by electrical currents) are highly selective and extremely rapid. A laser can remove ink from paper by vaporizing the ink while leaving the paper untouched.

Incredibly strong heat can be produced by a laser in places where mechanical contact is not possible. Lasers, therefore, can be used for small-scale precision cutting and welding and for delicate surgical operations. In fact, one of the earliest applications of lasers was for surgery on the retina of the eye.

Lasers in medicine and in certain industries—the textile business, for instance—generally are used because of their heat intensity and the flexibility and mobility with which this heat can be directed. Other applications of laser technology are opened up by its light-generating capacity. This characteristic allows lasers to carry information, increase computer memory storage capacity, and increase the speed with which large amounts of data can be calculated and manipulated.

In the year ahead, whole new categories of jobs will be created as laser technology is put to work in a variety of industries. Job titles such as "laser electro-optical technician," "gyro-optics technician," "laser specialist," "laser spectroscopists," and "laserists," although not household words, will become more familiar. Communications, information, and engineering areas will require increasingly greater numbers of technicians. In 1986, the number of laser-related jobs will grow.

INFORMATION MANAGEMENT MADE EASIER WITH LASERS

In recent years, personal computers have been made smaller and more powerful. Now the computer industry is on the verge of a second revolution—this one in computer memory capability. Optical laser-disks are about to make their debut for use with computers. Electronic buffs already are familiar with laser-disk technology used in compact audiodisks (see chapter 5) and video laser-disks. But with the introduction of twelve-inch disks for large computers (and, by 1986, smaller optical disks that microcomputers will be able to use), information storage and retrieval will take a giant leap forward.

Most magnetic disk drives in use today are capable of storing kilobytes or megabytes (thousands or millions of bytes) of data. Optical disks hold billions of bytes of information—gigabytes. Just one side of the twelve-inch optical disk can store 100 times more data than can be stored on the highest-capacity magnetic disk and 2,500 times more than on the lowest.

Like a phonograph record, a laser-disk contains information along thousands of circular tracks. To record data, however, laser light is aimed at the disk's metal layer, usually a gold-platinum alloy. Heat from the laser causes a micron-size bubble to rise. To retrieve data, the laser—at a lower power—scans the tracks.

Also like phonograph records, laser-disks can't be erased and reused. Once erasable optical storage is developed (many companies are working on it) and optical disks are made smaller for use with microcomputers, they'll have an enormous impact on information storage and retrieval. Government agencies, libraries, and data-processing firms—in fact, any business that manages and stores reams of information—no longer will need to warehouse miles of magnetic tapes or less durable and more cumbersome microfiche and microfilm. Optical laser-disks will provide them with compact, durable, and easily accessed filing systems.

Several companies, including Sony and Phillips, plan to sell laser-disk systems for retrieval of computer data. IBM and Apple are expected to announce similar products soon. Called CD-ROM (compact disc read-only memory), these systems will allow an astonishing quantity of information—encyclopedias, complete stock market records for past years, or collections of computer programs—to be instantly accessible to the home computer user.

LASERS LAUNCH A REVOLUTION IN EDUCATION AND TRAINING

Laser technology is revolutionizing the dissemination of information as well as its storage and retrieval. Laser computer printers, which are considerably quieter than their dot-matrix cousins, are becoming an office fixture. According to analysts at San Jose–based

Dataquest, a market research firm, sales of laser printers will triple by the end of 1986, to $2.5 billion.

From laser printers to laser-disks, this extraordinary technology is changing the way information is produced, packaged, and consumed. Within three years, Grolier Electronic Publishing Co. in New York will create a laser-disk encyclopedia on twenty-five disks, with thirty minutes per side for display on home TVs. According to Peter Cook, vice-president of creative services, the disks will not replicate the printed encyclopedia but will emphasize sound and images with films, pictures, maps, and graphs. Plans call for material to be arranged thematically, with sections such as arts, history, and sports. Because most American television sets can't display more than forty characters of text in large analog letters, a minimum of text will be used.

Notwithstanding the communications revolution, some things won't change. As Nicholas Negroponte, director of the media laboratory at MIT, points out, "In many regards, the old-fashioned book remains the best random-access information resource we have." Nevertheless, MIT's media laboratory has put together an electronic book. Using sound, motion films, and graphics to augment text, Negroponte and others created a continuously interactive format—as opposed to most videodisk systems which use a "your-turn, its-turn" format.

Called the movie manual, the MIT laser-disk and computing project combines digital text and analog pictures to guide users in repairing the automatic transmission of a car. Furnished with various choices on a touch-sensitive screen, the user at any point can ask for more information on a given subject while turning pages electronically. As one researcher describes the process, "The touch of a screen will cause a quarter-page illustration to burst into action as a sound-synchronized movie, demonstrating the transmission-repair process described in text on the same page. Or users can request that a black box or component in a schematic be opened up for examination."

Education and entertainment are becoming one and the same as interactive laser-disks, combined with computers—already widely used in industry and government—enter the consumer market.

Laser-disks use a laser beam of light to pick up coded signals embedded in the disk surface. Because nothing ever touches the disk surface, laser-disks last virtually forever. Their picture is the sharpest available for home use, and their stereo sound is as good as that of most audio-only components. Interactive laser-disks permit users to access any part of the disk in a random rather than a continuous format.

Educational laser-disks already are available in a variety of disciplines. Videodisc Publishing in New York sells a videodisk displaying some 1,650 paintings and sculptures of the Smithsonian's National Gallery of Art. The two-sided videodisk guides viewers through the museum, explains its history, and discusses the art. Romulus Productions Inc., New York City, has produced disks featuring the films *Citizen Kane* and *King Kong*, not only showing the movies but containing some 300 still frames that can be accessed to learn more about the scripts. The Vietnam War and a history quiz have been documented on disks by Starship Industries of Great Falls, Virginia.

Among the most popular subjects for educational laser-disks are science and technology. GPN, in Lincoln, Nebraska, distributes advanced high-school-level videodisks in biology, chemistry, and physics. John Wiley & Sons, in New York City, publishes a single-sided videodisk for math and physics education, called *The Puzzle of the Tacoma Narrows Bridge Collapse.* Videodisks are also available to teach foreign languages, and as reference and instructional manuals.

As yet no great works of literature have been put on laser-disks, although they probably will be. Among interactive disks, the most ambitious so far are those that let readers create the plot of a story. Two such books available are *Many Roads to Murder* and *Murder Anyone?*, both sold by Pioneer Videodisk, in Montvale, New Jersey.

BUSINESS BUYS INTO LASER-DISKS

Interactive laser-disks are gaining widespread acceptance as training tools in business and the military. Howell Training Co. of Houston, Texas, which trains oil company workers, recently started selling an interactive video program that simulates the controls of a refinery distillation tower. Howell president Thomas Cannaughton is convinced oil companies will pay $30,000 to put his system in their plant control rooms so workers can practice preventive-emergency procedures. Said Cannaughton, "Good training should be continuous. If you'd been trained by the Air Force to fly a sophisticated jet and then sent home for five years, you'd have problems."

Maynard, Massachusetts–based computer maker Digital Equipment began training workers with interactive video several years ago and last year started to market the system it developed. Digital found that workers learned lessons 40 percent faster with interactive video systems in their own offices than they did if they traveled to Digital's training facility and studied in more traditional classroom settings.

After years of experimentation, the Army is taking bids for 20,000 interactive video systems to be used to train personnel in repairing tanks and flying helicopters. By using interactive video, the instruction will cost much less than it would with real helicopters or million-dollar flight simulators.

A growing number of companies have adopted interactive laser-disks as marketing tools. Interactive Video Marketing Inc. (IVM) of Silver Spring, Maryland, recently introduced VuStar, a video laser-disk system that serves as a promotional tool for travel agencies. VuStar contains narrated video information on popular tourist spots, along with advertisements for hotels, restaurants, and shops. Tourist boards and local advertisers pay IVM for the space.

After years of advancing technology, interactive laser-disks are about to take off. Consumers and workers are being introduced to the technology in ordinary situations—on the job or in retail outlets—and are growing increasingly comfortable with it. NCR Corp., which recently introduced its InteracTV video systems, predicts that in 1986 customers will regularly be using such interactive video systems (see chapter 6).

In the year ahead, consumers increasingly will use credit cards protected with holograms to purchase products from interactive laser-disks. Holograms are created by a photographic process using a split laser beam that "sees" objects from several different vantage points. Because holograms can't be reproduced by ordinary photography, these cards are more difficult to counterfeit than ordinary printed pieces.

LASERS MAKE IT EASIER TO REACH OUT AND TOUCH SOMEONE

A $593-million fiber-optics cable—capable of carrying 37,800 telephone calls simultaneously on beams of laser light over hair-thin glass threads—is in the planning stages and involves AT&T and twenty-one other telecommunications companies. Final approval for the 7,200-mile system, stretching from California to Japan, awaits action by government agencies involved in the project. Approval is virtually guaranteed, and completion of the system is scheduled for 1988.

Within the United States, in 1984, some 35,000 miles of optical fibers were installed in New York City alone. Fiber-optics communications links already are in place between Boston and Washington, San Francisco and Bakersfield, California, and numerous other cities. In Houston, Southwestern Bell Telephone Co. will spend $76 million over the next three years to install 17,000 miles of light-guided cable and construct two digital switching centers to keep up with expected growth in data communications demand.

Besides contributing to the trans-Pacific fiber-optics link, AT&T will add 21,000 miles of fiber cables to its light-wave data communications system by 1990. Said Robert W. Kleinert, president and chief operating officer of AT&T Communications, "We intend to harness its tremendous power to meet our business and residential customers' growing needs for high-capacity, highly reliable voice, data, and video services." By 1988, he said, AT&T will send 1.7 billion pieces of data per second and transmit up to 169,000 simultaneous conversations.

Fiber-optics communications systems have come of age. Data communications analysts say that by the year 1990, fiber-optics networks will span the North American continent and the Atlantic and Pacific oceans. Linking cities separated by thousands of miles of land and oceans, as easily as cables link computers separated by a few office floors, fiber optics one day will relegate copper wires to museum showcases.

FIBER CABLES RIDE THE RAILS

Interestingly, optical-fiber fever is proving to be a boon for America's ailing railroads. With hundreds of miles of rights-of-way under their jurisdiction, the nation's railroads stand to earn millions of dollars from their sale. Instead of buying land and negotiating with countless property owners for the right to bury fiber-optics cable, companies like MCI, AT&T, and GTE-Sprint are reaching agreements with railroads.

In 1984, the Union Pacific System contracted with MCI, AT&T Communications interstate division, LDX Net Inc., and United Telecom Communications Inc. for 6,700 miles of right-of-way in fourteen states from Louisiana to Idaho. Now Norfolk Southern Railway and Santa Fe–Southern Pacific have formed a partnership —Fibertrak—to install their own 8,000-mile trunk line connecting San Francisco, Los Angeles, Chicago, New York, and other major cities at a cost of more than $1 billion. Said D. Henry Watts, chief executive officer of Fibertrak, "We decided that it was worth it to take some of the risk for the promise of a more handsome return."

As fiber-optics cable becomes the data communications channel of choice, makers of lasers and related devices also will reap handsome rewards. According to John Kessler, president of Kessler Marketing Intelligence, a market research firm in Newport, Rhode Island, the $96-million market in 1984 for lasers, light-emitting diodes, and similar devices used in fiber-optics systems will mushroom to $360 million by 1989.

LASERS WORK MEDICAL MAGIC

Concentrated beams of light have replaced the surgeon's knife for specialized tasks. By heating tissues, causing them to coagulate or fuse, ophthalmological lasers are useful in reconnecting detached retinas, removing birthmarks from skin, and removing tumors.

In the spring of 1985, the federal government granted approval for the use of lasers that travel within an optical fiber that is fine enough and flexible enough to be inserted into the body's natural openings. As a result, surgeons will be able to operate internally with considerably less trauma than in traditional surgery.

Known as YAG—for yttrium aluminum garnet—the fiber-optics lasers will prove invaluable to physicians for a variety of procedures. Lasers previously used in cataract surgery, for example, didn't solve the problem of membrane clouding behind the lens, which can cause blindness to recur even after cataracts have been removed. But by shining a beam of light from the YAG laser on the membrane, surgeons can vaporize it without opening the eye. A far less risky procedure, the YAG laser can be used in a physician's office rather than in a hospital, saving patients both time and money.

About 60 percent of bleeding ulcers can be controlled without surgery by using a YAG laser specifically designed for use in the stomach and intestines. Most people suffering from bleeding ulcers never need medical intervention, as bleeding stops spontaneously 80 percent of the time. However, about 100,000 victims a year are hospitalized, and 8 to 10 percent of them don't recover—a mortality rate that hasn't changed in thirty years. When emergency surgery is required for uncontrolled bleeding, the death rate increases to about 25 percent. By contrast, if the bleeding can be controlled nonsurgically, under nonemergency conditions, the mortality rate drops to about 3 percent.

YAGs also are used to treat patients with esophageal cancer. Frequently, such cancerous tumors prevent patients from swallowing. Burning a hole through the tumor with a laser opens the passageway. (It does not, unfortunately, cure the cancer.)

Millions of Americans have clogged arteries, which almost always lead to serious, and frequently fatal, heart disease. In 1984 alone, 200,000 patients required open-heart surgery to correct this condition. Soon a variation on the YAG concept will eliminate the need for coronary bypass surgery and balloon angioplasty (a procedure in which a balloon, inserted into the coronary artery through a catheter, compresses blockage and dilates artery walls to allow normal blood flow).

Called laser coronary angioplasty, the technique employs a laser attached to flexible glass fibers, encased in a catheter that is threaded through arteries to reach the plaque obstructing blood flow. The laser's energy is fired through the fibers, obliterating the plaque while avoiding the usual laser heat that can damage surrounding tissue.

Several groups of physicians and scientists are working on the technique. A team at New England Medical Center, led by Dr. Richard Cleveland, chief of surgery, first successfully used laser surgery on a human heart in 1983, and again in 1984. In both cases, the patients were suffering from a thickening of the heart's inner wall that made it impossible for their hearts to pump enough blood.

At the Cedars-Sinai Medical Center in Los Angeles and the Jet Propulsion Laboratory in Pasadena, researchers say they have succeeded in building a prototype device that will do what no previous design did: while vaporizing plaque at low temperatures, the fiber-optics laser produces a video image of the blockage so that physicians can see the plaque before blasting it. The researchers say that their device can be threaded through smaller arteries than previous devices could manage. Plaque more commonly collects in these smaller arteries.

Although new technology has a tendency to drive up health costs, lasers will bring costs down. Coronary bypass surgery costs about $20,000 a person. Many of those patients are candidates for less invasive techniques, including laser angioplasty. If the technique were widely available, many victims would have the procedure done in a physician's office or surgicenter and go home the same day.

In the year ahead, researchers will continue to develop and perfect medical applications for laser technology. At the Mayo Clinic, a forty-year-old procedure has been given a computer-assisted update. Three-dimensional "road maps," to navigate deep into a patient's brain during surgery to pinpoint tumors, have long been possible. Using what is known as stereotaxi—determining where straight lines would intersect if drawn from three points on the skull—surgeons have pinpointed tumor locations. Today, those "road maps" are being drawn by computers that guide a laser beam more precisely than is possible manually. Because the computer-assisted stereotactic procedure can be performed through a much smaller opening in the skull, and with less disturbance of brain tissue, patients do better and have fewer neurological aftereffects than in conventional surgery.

Use of computers to locate tumors and other disorders in the brain, say scientists, eventually will lead to robots in the operating room. In the not-too-distant future, computers and lasers together will perform a mind-boggling array of medical miracles. By the year 2000, predicts Dr. Sabastian Arena, head of the microsurgery laboratory at Mercy Hospital in Pittsburgh, surgeons will be able to switch a person's fertility on and off, operate on fetuses in the womb, and remove, repair, and replace body organs, all courtesy of surgery employing computers, holograms, laser beams, and miniature multipurpose instruments.

FROM STAR WARS TO GROUND WARS

In April 1985, officials dedicated the world's most powerful laser, a technological wonder that scientists believe will lead to a cheap, safe way of making electricity. Planned and constructed by over 300 companies, and housed in Lawrence Livermore National Laboratory in Livermore, California, the $176-million NOVA laser will be used by researchers attempting to weld the nuclei of hydrogen atoms in order to release bursts of energy at temperatures exceeding those at the sun's center. (Before its dedication, the NOVA already had set a laser power record—57 trillion watts—in scientists' quest to harness nuclear fusion as an energy source.)

NOVA also could be used to improve thermonuclear bombs by mimicking certain reactions in a controlled laboratory setting. It is likely to be used in research for the "Star Wars" defense program.

When the space shuttle *Discovery* went up in June 1985, it conducted the first Star Wars experiment in orbit. A mirror attached to the shuttle intercepted and reflected a laser beam fired from earth. The laser, weakened so it wouldn't damage the spacecraft, was aimed from an Air Force base on Maui, Hawaii, and bounced back by a special eight-inch-diameter "retroreflector."

The use of ground-based lasers is one of several options that the Pentagon's Strategic Defense Initiative (SDI) office is evaluating to decide whether an antimissile system is feasible. The antimissile plan is expected to combine space- and ground-based devices in a complex system to intercept and destroy ballistic missiles.

In the not-too-distant future, a new generation of laser-equipped robots will be available for ground-war operations. Currently being developed at Carnegie-Mellon University in Pittsburgh, the Terragator is, essentially, a car with six wheels and television cameras. It propels itself and needs no driver. The Terragator uses a combination of lasers, sonar devices, and stereo television with multiple cameras to scan the terrain and react accordingly.

In theory, the straight lines, undulations, curves, curbs, and edges that are normal features of roads can be seen, and instructions for steering and speed adjustments are made automatically. If sensors confront extremely complicated patterns, the Terragator communicates with a larger, mainframe computer programmed with a wider variety of visual scenarios.

Although a long way from perfection, such vehicles may one day go where others fear to tread—into radioactive factories, for instance, or into battle. One idea being contemplated by the Army is called the "mother and ducklings" scenario. A single manned tank would lead a squadron of unmanned robot tanks. While in formation, the squadron would take commands from the manned tank. Once in battle, each tank would operate independently. According to a Pentagon report on strategic computing, "Autonomous land vehicle systems could support such missions as deep-penetration of reconnaissance, rear area resupply, ammunition handling, and weapons delivery."

In the year ahead, new applications of laser technology will continue to make the extraordinary ordinary. All of us will be touched by lasers in some way—at home, in the office, in the hospital, at play, or just going about our daily chores. How many of us actually will see the light? Not many. Most lasers are packaged into products, not independent of them. So, unlike computers, which most of us had to get used to, lasers will insinuate themselves into our lives without our knowing it.

8 *PRIVATE ENTERPRISE* *TAKES A CHUNK OUT* OF GOVERNMENT. *DISCOVERING PROFIT* *IN SCHOOLS, TRANSIT* *SYSTEMS, PRISONS.*

The city of Newark, New Jersey, pays private industry to clean the sewers, repair streets, maintain municipal vehicles, and provide specialty printing and data processing. Los Angeles County has signed 139 contracts with private companies, mostly for park and grounds maintenance. In Phoenix, Arizona, city departments bid against private companies and contractors to provide many city-financed services, including janitorial services, trash collection, and major street landscaping.

At some small airports—such as those in Enid, Oklahoma, and North Myrtle Beach, South Carolina—the Federal Aviation Administration no longer staffs control towers. The FAA provides funds so that local authorities can hire entrepreneurs to control air traffic. And in Arizona and Georgia, several communities are served wholly or in part by private fire departments.

Privatization—the private delivery of public services—is sweeping the nation. Egged on by the Reagan administration and encouraged by reported savings of better than 20 percent over publicly administered programs in some communities, mayors and county officials are turning to private industry to provide a wide range of public services.

Garbage collection tasks and street maintenance were the first areas to be privatized. Now prisons, hospitals, and public transportation networks are being put in the hands of private operators. What's next? Education. For-profit tutoring, adult continuing education courses, and executive learning centers are cropping up around the country, as entrepreneurs and established corporations rush to fill a gap created by widespread public dissatisfaction with America's educational system.

In the year ahead, a steady trickle of private companies assuming once-public tasks for profit will become a downpour. Entrepreneurs and established corporations alike will eagerly bid for government contracts as both government and business realize that reprivatization can be a win-win proposition for local communities.

AN OLD IDEA WHOSE TIME HAS COME

Recent publicity aside, the idea behind privatization is not all that new. Government administrators—federal, state, and local—have long vacillated between providing services themselves and contracting them out. In the early 1900s, for example, privately operated fire departments, toll roads, bridges, streetcar systems, and garbage collection services were commonplace. Then corruption set in. The era of big-city political bosses led to abuses as municipal contracts became a popular form of patronage. In many cities, payoffs by contractors became commonplace, services deteriorated, and contractors overcharged.

In the 1920s, communities decided to professionalize the delivery of public services by making them part of the municipal government. Now, say political analysts, the pendulum is swinging back. Noted Dr. A. Lee Fritschler, director of the Center for Public Policy Education at the Brookings Institution in Washington, D.C.: "We seem to go through these swings. When the marketplace doesn't work well, we let government do it. And when government doesn't work well, we go back to the private sector."

A few clear-cut considerations explain this all-consuming passion to reprivatize government services. In the 1960s and 1970s, the federal government sharply increased funds to the cities; cities in turn could increase services without increasing taxes. The expansion of political power by extending services—thus creating new jobs and constituencies—gained momentum. In recent years, as the flood of federal dollars dwindled to a trickle, municipalities found themselves burdened with expensive, troublesome public service responsibilities they could not meet without raising taxes. In a decidedly antitax environment, contracting became an attractive alternative.

Nationally, private industry now provides local governments with a significant fraction of an incredible array of services. According to the International City Management Association, 41 percent of all commercial solid-waste collection and 34 percent of residential collection are done by private contractors. In health services, 25 percent of once publicly managed hospitals is now administered by private firms. Some 48 percent of municipal legal services is provided by private concerns. Highest of all is the percentage of vehicle towing and storage operations that have been transferred to the private sector: 78 percent.

Reprivatization of public services affects cities large and small. It occurs more slowly in large, heavily unionized northeastern cities, and more quickly in fast-growing cities of the West and Southwest. Supporters of the movement insist that private companies can perform many services more efficiently by circumventing government bureaucracy and political considerations. Moreover, costs are lowered through bulk purchasing and personnel reductions and by paying lower salaries and benefits.

Others insist that infusing the public sector with private industry-style competition forces public agencies to become more efficient—that privatization actually enhances the accountability of local government. Said Mayor George Latimer of St. Paul, where private industry provides sanitation, street paving, sewers, lighting improvement, and other services: "Private contracts act as a good discipline on our own operations. It gives local government more flexibility."

PRIVATIZATION SAVES MONEY

Another avid supporter is County Executive Dalton Roberts of Hamilton County, Tennessee, which includes Chattanooga. Roberts points out that cities "decide the level of service to be provided" and that the "No. 1 feature is, [privatization] saves us money."

Critics, on the other hand, worry that a sweeping move to reprivatize is a thinly disguised attempt to abdicate government responsibility. They contend that this trend will reduce services for society's wards, take jobs from public employees, and open the door to abuses by private companies. Already, complaints are coming from civil liberty and minority groups that for-profit corrections companies are cutting corners in handling prisoners and alien detainees.

Public employee unions, among the strongest opponents of privatization, aver that private companies can do the job more cheaply only because they pay low wages, offer services only in select, profitable areas, and make no attempt to meet social obligations such as minority hiring or contracting with small businesses. Many warn that private companies, if threatened with profit losses, simply will abandon nonprofitable segments of their business, leaving areas without service.

Whether pro or con, virtually all political observers agree that in transferring public services to private control, local governments are redefining their role. They're making a distinction between setting policy—including minimum level of service—and actually providing services. In effect, governments are telling constituents that they can't be everything to everybody—that their responsibility is to see that services are made available, but not to provide them.

Propagated by entrepreneurial enthusiasm, companies taking over public services no longer are small upstarts with more energy than capital. Sprawling, publicly owned corporations, with financial assistance from major Wall Street institutions, now join entrepreneurs in eager anticipation of an acceleration of federal privatization efforts and additional federal budget cuts, which will force state and local governments to turn even more of their services over to the private sector.

By any measure, the currents of reprivatization are strong and getting stronger. Since 1980, eleven private corrections companies and more than two dozen private firefighting companies have set up operations. At least eight private companies operate air traffic control towers—up from four in 1980. More than a dozen companies have signed or proposed deals to build, own, and operate municipal waste-water treatment plants—all have emerged in the past two years. Hundreds of other companies trim trees in public parks, maintain streetlights, and collect trash.

FEDERAL GOVERNMENT ENDORSES PRIVATIZATION

Reprivatization is not the sole province of local governments. The Reagan administration heartily endorses private operation of public facilities. And in the fall of 1984, federal officials adopted new rules making it easier to replace government functions with contract services. Meanwhile, the federal government is negotiating to sell Conrail, the freight line, and Landsat, the weather-mapping satellite, to private interests. It also is pushing to put veterans in non-VA hospitals and is experimenting with plans to sell public-housing apartments to tenants in hope that private ownership will improve the projects' maintenance.

In 1981, federal authorities began turning over control tower operations at small airports. Under the program, federal funds are given to local governments which, in turn, contract with private air traffic control operators. Cost savings have been significant. Average cost of a one-year private contract is about $150,000, as compared to about $220,000 for an FAA-operated tower.

Cost savings are realized chiefly through lower salaries—significantly lower. Starting salaries for an air traffic controller with a private firm can be less than $10,000 a year. The FAA pays $17,000 to start and reaches $32,000. Private companies also are free to hire part-time controllers, a practice prohibited under federal regulations.

BIRTH OF A PRIVATE INDUSTRY

In 1982, the private waste-water treatment industry was born. After the federal government began phasing out its huge program of grants for plant construction, a whole new industry emerged.

Already federal support funds have been pared from a peak funding of $4.5 billion a year to $2.4 billion. Despite the cuts, federal clean-water rules have not been eased, and thousands of U.S. towns and cities are considering private plants for the savings they offer. Providing contractors' funds by floating municipal industrial development bonds at favorable rates keeps capital relatively cheap.

Furthermore, private companies can take advantage of investment tax credits and accelerated depreciation. They do not need to comply with federal minimum wage or minority hiring or contracting rules. Consequently, construction time is halved. Among active promoters of the new industry are major accounting firms such as Arthur Young & Co., which has served as consultant on such deals, and municipal bond underwriters such as Shearson Lehman American Express, E. F. Hutton, and Smith Barney.

In response to criticism that such plants interest private investors only because of sizable federal tax breaks, an Arthur Young & Co. representative acknowledged that private waste-water treatment plants are attractive because of federal tax breaks. But he also pointed out that the plants pay local property taxes, unlike government-owned facilities.

Some $15 billion in annual operating expenditures that could be privatized have been identified by the federal Office of Management and Budget. The President's Private Sector Survey Council—more commonly called the Grace Commission, after its chairman, J. Peter Grace—makes even grander forecasts. It says the government could save an incredible $11.2 billion over a three-year period simply by turning the two federal airports outside Washington—National and Dulles—over to the private sector.

Whatever the motive, the private sector is rushing in where municipal governments no longer can afford to tread. The service providers are reaping substantial profits, but are they providing better service? Some aren't, most are.

INCARCERATION NOW A PRIVATE AFFAIR

Behavioral Systems Southwest Inc. in Pasadena, California, has converted an old convalescent home into a short-term holding facility for up to 125 aliens awaiting deportation by the Immigration and Naturalization Service (INS). The firm also operates a similar facility in Aurora, Colorado.

Nashville-based Corrections Corp. of America operates five facilities, including the nation's first privately operated county jail, in Hamilton County, Tennessee, and detention centers built for the INS in Houston and Laredo. In 1984, Corrections Corp. charged the INS $23.84 a day per detainee at the Houston facility, compared to the average $26.45 a day it costs the U.S. government to house deportees. Corrections Corp.'s charges also include capital costs, while the INS figure covers only operating costs. Furthermore, the corporation used its own equity to fund the $4.3-million construction costs and completed the minimum-security facility in 1983, in six months' time—three years sooner than the INS would have. Because of cumbersome review and approval procedures, the INS could not have completed the facility before 1986.

Lewisburg, Pennsylvania–based Buckingham Security Ltd. has bought land in North Sewick Township, Pennsylvania, outside Pittsburgh, on which it plans to build a $25-million 700-bed maximum-security prison. A similar facility is planned for Gooding, Idaho. Buckingham intends to house protective custody inmates and other low-risk prisoners requiring maximum security.

Protective custody accounts for about 7 percent, or 35,000, of the nation's prison population. This is the largest segment of what are considered "special needs" prisoners. (Other special needs groups are the mentally or emotionally handicapped and the elderly.) Recently, judges have ruled that housing protective custody inmates with "hardened criminals" is tantamount to cruel and unusual punishment. To protect them, they must be locked up in the most secure cells—of necessity, in solitary confinement usually reserved for incorrigibles. Said Joseph Fenton, executive vice-president of Buckingham and a real estate entrepreneur, "The courts, more and more, lean in the direction that just because you are in protective custody doesn't mean you shouldn't be given the treatment of the best-behaved prisoner."

Public resistance explains why Buckingham chose two economically depressed communities in which to build its facilities. When Gooding's packing plant was closed, many jobs were lost in this largely agrarian Idaho community. Although the community insisted that Buckingham house only protective custody and other low-risk inmates, the local business community is "doing everything possible to make sure this deal goes through," noted Bradley Blum, editor of the Gooding County *Leader.* He added that "while there are some people who aren't too crazy about the idea, no one is speaking against an idea that will bring 350 jobs to town."

Economics is a powerful incentive for local governments to turn prison facilities over to private industry, and it's an equally strong incentive for private industry to assume the role of jailer. Donaldson, Lufkin & Jenrette, a Wall Street brokerage house, calls corporate-run jails "a new growth industry."

Today, nearly as many Americans are behind bars (663,000) as live in San Francisco (678,000). Among industrialized nations, only the Soviet Union and South Africa have imprisoned a larger share of their populations. Tougher sentencing laws in virtually all fifty states have doubled the jail and prison population since 1975. And over the next decade, taxpayers will spend $6 billion to $7 billion to build cells—and tens of billions more to operate them. Incarceration is, indeed, a high-growth industry.

With growth virtually guaranteed, private firms that contract to design, build, and operate prisons, as well as those that finance prison bond sales and investors who collect the tax-exempt interest on them, are certain to earn handsome profits. Injecting private ownership into prisons, insist proponents, will do for the prison industry what private ownership has done for the hospital business —make it more competitive.

Despite unanswered questions about who chases escapees and who is liable for prisoners' well-being while in jail or while being transported from prison to court and back, privately operated prisons are certain to become a fixture of the criminal justice system in the year ahead.

PRIVATE COMPANIES GIVE MASS TRANSIT A LIFT

James Williams's combination bus, cab, and van service, Tidewater Transit, provides Portsmouth, Virginia, residents with cheaper, more convenient service than the troubled Tidewater Transit Transportation Commission was able to offer. In Chicago, huge fare increases a few years ago led many suburban commuters to form bus pools run without subsidy by a private operator. After pulling out of the city's regional transit agency, a Kansas City, Missouri, suburb switched to a private operator to run its bus system. And suburbs around Columbus, Ohio, are testing the use of taxis as feeders to public transit stops.

Around the country, private operators are taking over public transit systems. They fare particularly well where centralized public transit systems have faltered—in the suburbs—by gearing services to the now dominant, suburb-to-suburb travel patterns of today's commuters. While public transit systems have watched costs soar and ridership stagnate, private operators have proved adept at tailoring their services to the suburbs' fragmented travel patterns.

Paramus, New Jersey's Enterprise Transit Corp., for instance, eliminates transfers by using small buses to transport groups of commuters carefully selected according to where they live and work. One New York stockbroker, who used to take three trains from her Fort Lee, New Jersey, home to her job in Manhattan, now rides one Enterprise bus directly. The fare is only $15 more than the $120 a month she paid for New Jersey Transit service. The bus also offers such amenities as the morning newspaper, reclining seats, and individual reading lights.

Like many other systems, Cleveland's Regional Transit Authority (RTA) has lost nearly a third of its riders since 1980. Authority officials attribute the losses to rising fares, service cutbacks, poor service, high unemployment, and continuing population shifts to outlying areas. In an attempt to diversify its service and recoup some of its losses, RTA is considering a variety of approaches: contracting with taxi companies in outlying areas to drive commuters to bus or rapid transit lines; leasing vans to groups of riders or to employers who turn them over to their employees; contracting with private operators to provide publicly subsidized transit service; providing dial-a-ride services; and offering "subscription buses," chartered by employers to pick up and transport workers from central locations.

Private transit systems are not a new idea. Until the late 1950s, private involvement in community transportation was commonplace. In New York, for example, private investors built and operated the network of buses, subways, and elevated trains. After World War II, the system fell on hard times as affluent city dwellers moved to the suburbs and began relying on private automobiles and an ever-expanding highway system. By 1960, most transit systems across the country had been taken over by local governments.

Now federal transportation support funds have all but dried up—with another $2.7 billion on operating subsidies scheduled to be phased out over three years. Public transit officials are reassessing their role and the role of business in the delivery of transportation services, including the planning of city transit systems. In Hartford, Connecticut, for example, businesses helped pay for a regional transportation study and then coordinated efforts to impose the study's recommendations for van pooling, downtown parking restrictions, and flexible work hours to reduce peak-hour traffic congestion.

Despite strong opposition from transportation workers' unions, who fear loss of jobs to nonunionized private contractors and warn that private transit companies will not serve unprofitable lower-income areas, public officials are openly embracing the reprivatization of transportation. In San Diego, officials allow twelve companies to operate forty jitneys or vans on semifixed routes. Westchester County, New York, has long-term contracts with six companies for more than 320 buses, which carry 100,000 passengers daily. Operating costs are less than half of New York City's buses. At least twenty-two cities—including Pittsburgh, Chattanooga, Miami, Chicago, Berkeley, and San Francisco—have deregulated transit systems to permit at least limited jitney service and more competitive taxi service. And peak-hour congestion, one of the more troublesome urban transit problems, is relieved in Boston, Chicago, New York, and San Francisco by limited private-subscription bus service.

As annual operating deficits mount, public officials realize that public and private roles must mesh to meet public transportation needs. Glamorous, bureaucratized, high-cost, high-speed development plans are giving way to the "ugly duckling" approach—decentralized, locally tailored, competitive transit.

PRIVATIZATION TAKES ON GLOBAL PROPORTIONS

In 1980, Southend-on-Sea, a city at the mouth of the Thames, hired a private garbage collector, setting off a chain reaction that led to municipalities contracting for services at the rate of about one a day. Said Madsen Pirie, president of the Adam Smith Institute in London, a free-enterprise-minded research foundation: "We estimate the local governments save about 25 percent annually by hiring private contractors." A private window-cleaning service at Hull, in Yorkshire, saves the local school 80 percent over the costs of such service by public employees.

British localities—and governments around the world—are discovering what their American counterparts have learned: A local authority is not necessarily an ideal business unit, and a governmental work force is not necessarily better or cheaper than a private work force. Now, as the British government sells off nationalized companies to private investors—a dozen large state-owned companies have been turned over to the private sector thus far—and local governments privatize services from rat catching to school meals, Margaret Thatcher's Tories hope to put laws through Parliament forcing local authorities to take bids on services.

As in the United States, British trade unions have launched a campaign against privatization. To support their position, they've issued a report full of "horror stories," tales of monumental failures by private firms performing once-public services. Nonetheless the trend continues apace.

In South Korea, the state has divested itself of five large commercial banks, an oil company, and a heavy industrial enterprise. Canada's Progressive Conservative government scheduled for early sale Nordair Ltd., a regional airline; Northern Transportation Co., a northern Canadian shipping and trucking firm; and Eldorado Nuclear Co., a major uranium producer and processor, all in an effort to reduce the state's involvement in the Canadian economy.

In March 1985, the West German Cabinet approved Finance Minister Gerhard Stoltenberg's plan for partial and gradual reprivatization of five companies: Volkswagen; Viag AG, Germany's major aluminum producer; Prakla-Seismos GmbH, a flourishing geological survey and exploration company; and two banks. Even France's socialist government has decided to allow subsidiaries of major industrial companies nationalized in 1982 to sell some equity to the public. Not exactly a sweeping privatization effort, but dramatic considering whence it came.

Bangladesh and Pakistan have denationalized a number of jute, textile, cotton ginning, rice, and flour mills which previous governments had nationalized. Even China, Hungary, and a handful of other communist countries are privatizing operations of state companies, albeit in a limited way.

Why is this happening? In many cases, it's because the government simply cannot afford the huge operating deficits of state-owned companies. In other instances, privatization or reprivatization is politically motivated. But for most governments, it's a long-term growth strategy—a bottom-line consideration. There is widespread recognition that nations which have relied most on competition and free markets have made greater economic progress in recent decades. Industrialized countries and third-world nations alike would like to duplicate that success.

FOR-PROFIT EDUCATION CATCHING ON

Occurring not by legislative fiat but by consumer demand, for-profit education is exploding. According to a report issued by the Carnegie Foundation for the Advancement of Teaching, *Corporate Classrooms: The Learning Business,* nearly $60 billion a year is spent on corporate-run education, about "the cost of the nation's four-year colleges and universities, both public and private." The number of employees involved in corporate education is nearly equal to total enrollment of those same institutions—about 8 million students.

IBM alone spends $700 million a year on education for its employees. Xerox Corp., RCA Corp., Holiday Inns Inc., and other companies have built their own educational facilities, many of which resemble in every way a college campus, with dormitories, classrooms, and recreational centers. The Wang Institute of

Graduate Studies, for example, occupies a former seminary on a 200-acre site along the Merrimack River in rural Tyngsboro, Massachusetts.

At least eighteen corporations and industry-wide associations such as the Institute of Textile Technology in Charlottesville, Virginia, award academic degrees that are, or soon will be, recognized by regional accrediting agencies. Eight more have plans to do so by 1988. Although generally limited to company employees, some corporate coursework is available to the public. The Rand Corp., for instance, offers a Ph.D. program to both employees and nonemployees. Some corporate colleges have long histories, but most have cropped up in the past few years.

"Satellite universities" soon will join the ranks of corporate-run educational programs. Created by IBM, Westinghouse Corp., Digital Equipment Corp., and others, the National Technological University will broadcast courses via satellites to corporate classrooms around the country.

Corporate-run educational programs challenge traditional educational facilities. To compete, said Edward L. Boyer, former U.S. commissioner of education and current president of the Carnegie Foundation, "traditional institutions may have to learn from the efficiency, flexibility, and clear sense of purpose of their new corporate competitors." He also warned that in attempting to be more competitive, traditional institutions may abandon academics for careerism. In that event, "higher education may discover that, having abandoned its own special mission, it will find itself in a contest it cannot win."

PARENTS TURN TO FOR-PROFIT TUTORING CENTERS

Once the exclusive territory of schools, counseling and remedial education services are now being offered by private businesses around the country. Founded by a former California schoolteacher, the Sylvan Learning Corp. has 140 franchises throughout the country. Offering individual attention that public schools cannot afford, and using teaching techniques appropriate to a student's special needs, these for-profit educational centers specialize in teaching basic skills in mathematics and reading.

In a few areas, entire school districts are contracting with these educational entrepreneurs to provide alternative classes for potential school dropouts or for students whose basic skills need improvement. In virtually every state, parents of children with learning problems, and others disillusioned with the quality of education in public schools, pay as much as $26 dollars an hour twice a week to ensure faster improvement and better achievement test scores.

Some centers are independent, some members of corporate chains, and others part of a national franchise. All are reaping huge profits from widespread dissatisfaction among parents. Critics argue that the high cost of such programs will widen the gap between middle-class students, whose families can afford extra help, and those who need it most—poor, minority, and learning-handicapped students. Harvard Professor Harold Howe, a former U.S. commissioner of education, notes: "One problem with privatization is that there is a tendency for the profit motive to short-change the people who have the most difficult problems or the least resources."

Criticism has done little to dampen consumers' enthusiasm. Since opening in 1970, California-based American Learning Corp. has enrolled 100,000 students in the West and Midwest, with an annual net profit of 5 to 9 percent.

In the year ahead, the reprivatization of America will become a swollen tide of private industry rushing in to fill the gaps left by federal government budget cuts, local governments' inability to finance basic public services, and consumer demand for quality service and greater accountability.

9 MADISON AVENUE REMOLDS THE PROFESSIONS. REMOVING THE MYSTIQUE FROM MEDICINE AND LAW.

Until recently, two commonly held precepts remained constant in the public mind: Economists and weather forecasters were always wrong, and doctors and lawyers were always right—or if not right, at least better equipped to deal with the human condition than ordinary mortals. During the past few years, one of those precepts has been shattered. Increasingly, doctors and lawyers are being viewed as all too human. Nationwide, medical malpractice suits have tripled in the last decade, and million-dollar verdicts have become commonplace. A 1983 Gallup Poll surveying people's attitudes about the honesty and ethical standards of 25 occupations ranked lawyers thirteenth—sandwiched between newspaper reporters and stockbrokers.

Plummeting prestige—which both doctors and lawyers blame on the media's inclination to emphasize, and sensationalize, the darker side of professional conduct while ignoring more positive, altruistic activities—may be disconcerting. But revolutionary changes in the marketplace will prove to be a much more difficult hurdle to overcome.

The days of walking out of professional training programs and into lucrative private practices are over. In the year ahead, physicians, dentists, and lawyers will be forced to embrace marketplace survival strategies. In 1986, most independent professionals and group practitioners will advertise, specialize, and computerize to stay afloat.

MARKET GLUT CREATES COMPETITIVE ENVIRONMENT

Darwin's survival-of-the-fittest theory never was more appropriately applied than in the current competitive environment for doctors and lawyers. In sheer numbers, they are an overwhelming presence. As of 1984, there were 622,000 lawyers in the country—2.5 lawyers for every 1,000 people. (In bellwether Florida, the number of lawyers qualified to practice increased by 120 percent between 1973 and 1983.) Similarly, about 500,000 physicians practice in the United States, 70,000 more than needed. Currently, there are 2 doctors for every 1,000 people, according to Columbia University economist Eli Ginsberg. By the year 2000, there will be 3 doctors for every 1,000 people, representing a surplus of 145,000 doctors.

Nevertheless, medical and law school graduates continue to flood the market. Although recent enrollment declines will significantly reduce the number of professionals entering the market, that impact won't be felt for at least a decade. Meanwhile, some 30,000 new physicians and lawyers will leave school this year, looking for a place to hang their shingles.

How will they survive in an economic environment that has already witnessed a sharp drop in income levels for first-year professionals? By learning the same skills that all business people must learn. Whether signing on with a corporation, joining a well-established group practice, forming a new one, or going it alone, doctors and lawyers will be confronted with some harsh realities. A decade of consumer activism has created a market in which quality is paramount, accountability is enforced, and educated consumers shop for the most cost-effective service.

LAWYERS AND DOCTORS ADOPT MADISON AVENUE

To be competitive, even the most hard-line traditionalists are letting Madison Avenue set the tone. In 1977, the U.S. Supreme Court struck down the ban on lawyer advertising. Since then, 14 percent of the country's 60,000-plus lawyers have turned to advertising. According to the American Bar Assn., 82 percent of those who tried advertising were satisfied with the results.

Promotional campaigns for attorneys have gone beyond inserting business cards in specialized publications. Blue-chip corporate law firms now market themselves through glossy brochures, special reports, and seminars. Some firms aggressively target specific clients. The Berman law firm in Minneapolis, for example, ran an ad in *The Wall Street Journal* to attract dissatisfied investors. The ad read, "Have You Lost Money Because You Were Misled?" A law firm in Milwaukee—Habush, Habush & Davis—runs television spots telling skiers how to bring damage suits.

Jacoby & Meyers, one of the nation's biggest legal clinics, runs client-specific television advertisements targeted to viewing audiences. Late-night ads, for instance, are designed to draw divorce cases, and ads during afternoon soap operas attract Social Security cases. Legal clinics, a fast-growing segment of the law profession, promote their services in much the same way medical emergicenters promote theirs. They also offer supermarket-style specialties, selling divorce or bankruptcy counsel for as little as $35 to $75.

In 1982, Columbus, Ohio, lawyer Philip Q. Zauderer ran an ad in local newspapers reading: "Did you use this IUD?" The ad featured a picture of A. H. Robin Co.'s Dalkon Shield, which many women insist has caused them problems. Zauderer was promptly called before the Ohio Supreme Court and reprimanded for violating a state rule that prohibits lawyers from making specific product or company-oriented pitches to win clients.

On May 28, 1985, a divided U.S. Supreme Court overruled the Ohio court, declaring that the decision impinged on the lawyer's free-speech rights. Writing the majority opinion, Associate Justice

Byron R. White noted that Zauderer's ads "tended to acquaint persons with their legal rights who might otherwise be shut off from effective access to the legal system."

Advertising may well acquaint persons with their legal rights, but that decision is certain to accelerate the pace of advertising among attorneys. Critics of this trend claim such ads result in expensive lawsuits that line the pockets of lawyers, not people with problems. Banks complain that lawyers advertising debt liquidation are fueling a surge in personal bankruptcy. Manufacturers assert that they have been overburdened with new product liability and worker's compensation claims that can be directly attributed to product or company-specific advertisements.

To be sure, many lawyers share the opinion of Associate Justice Sandra Day O'Connor that lawyers should live up to "standards beyond those prevailing in the marketplace." Perhaps they should, but the reality of the marketplace in the year ahead will dictate otherwise.

PHYSICIAN, SELL THYSELF

Physicians, too, are being forced to advertise their wares with a hard-sell approach traditionally associated with toothpaste and laundry detergent. Until only a few years ago, it was considered unprofessional, and bordering on the unethical, for physicians to advertise. Today a glimpse at the Yellow Pages tells the story. Pages that used to contain a list of doctors now are filled with display ads promoting individual doctors, group practices, emergicenters, and hospital programs.

In 1983, the U.S. Supreme Court ruled that the American Medical Assn. (AMA) no longer could prohibit doctors from advertising, finding the policy to be equivalent to a free-trade restriction. Shortly afterward, ads began appearing in newspapers and on radio and television. Banner headlines, such as "Here's Important News About Cataract Laser Surgery" and "Nearsighted? In-Office Surgery to Reduce Nearsightedness (Myopia)," and promotions offering reduced-cost one-day surgical procedures sparked a controversy that has yet to subside.

Many physicians decry the introduction of advertising and selling techniques into the medical field. They claim it is unethical and runs counter to the notion that doctors should build their practices only by providing good care to those who seek their services, not by soliciting patients through slick public relations campaigns. Controversy or no, advertising among physicians will become standard practice as competition for patients heats up.

Pressure to reduce health costs while maintaining a full patient load will force many practitioners to advertise. This is true of dentists, no less than medical doctors, but dentists face an additional problem. As more people take advantage of preventive remedies and use fluoridated water, cavities become a problem of the past. Yet dental schools are turning out graduates at a rapid clip. So first-year dentists are following in the footsteps of M.D.s, joining established practices or contracting with dental clinics rather than starting out on their own.

As competition increases, professionals begin to realize they must market their services in much the same way that nonservice businesses marketed their products. Advertising in all its facets not only is permissible, but in some cases necessary for survival. In the year ahead, virtually all promotional limits will be lifted. Any advertising other than deceptive advertising not only will be acceptable, it will be expected—and quite respectable.

To be sure, most professional schools don't teach marketing. Yet. Consequently, doctors, dentists, and attorneys are hiring trained marketing personnel, skilled in the fine art of selling. When Dr. Robert Fenton, a Detroit radiologist, realized he wasn't seeing any growth in his practice, he did what doctors are trained to do with difficult cases. He called in a specialist. In this case, the specialist was a marketing consultant.

On the advice of his consultant, Dr. Fenton now markets his services directly to the public, rather than relying on referrals by other physicians. He also operates two well-advertised walk-in breast-exam clinics, where, for $190, a woman can receive a complete cancer screen and walk out two hours later with the results. At first, Dr. Fenton's colleagues were skeptical. Now they call to ask how he did it.

A group of Baton Rouge ophthalmologists also turned to a marketing consultant. Determining that their patients came from two distinct population groups, the consultant planned two very different advertising campaigns. One campaign, emphasizing the latest in high-tech eye care, was targeted toward married women between the ages of eighteen and forty-five, who make most medical decisions for their husbands and children. The second campaign, a soft-sell approach, was geared toward older patients, reminding them about the pleasure they receive in seeing their grandchildren. Both campaigns attracted new patients.

Walk-in health-care clinics now are as common as fast-food restaurants. So common, in fact, that they have come to be known as "Docs in the Boxes" (see chapter 3). Similarly, in 1986, "McDentists" and "McLawyers" will dot the landscape, as richly paneled office motifs give way to the shopping mall look and location.

More and more dentists are joining together in group practices, sharing office space, staff, and equipment and, by so doing, economizing on capital investment requirements. For consumers, it means the availability of comprehensive dental care in a single location at lower cost. In many areas, such multispecialty clinics already are thriving.

Not to be outdone by medical HMOs, dental services also are available on a subscriber basis. With names like Denti-Plan, Compdent Dental Plan, Caps Dental Plan, and Safeguard Health Plan, dental services are offered on the same basis as an HMO or a preferred provider organization.

REACHING OUT FOR CLIENTS

Conveniently located legal clinics are perhaps the fastest-growing segment of legal services, as attorneys scramble to become the H&R Blocks of law. The two largest—Jacoby & Meyers, with 140 offices in six states, and Hyatt Legal Services, with 161 offices in twenty states—have become the standard against which other aspiring clinics measure themselves.

In an effort to compete, private-practice attorneys are insinuating themselves onto clinic turf. One Clearwater, Florida, attorney,

Daniel Gianini, grossed $400,000 in 1984 by drafting wills, settling divorce cases, and defending clients in traffic and criminal cases from his conveniently located shopping mall office. Said Gianini, "I think attorneys being more accessible is an idea that has to come. In this competitive market, you must reach out to your market and grab it. We try to make it as convenient as possible to come in and ask questions."

Convenience is a key to survival for all professional service providers. Some doctors, and even dentists, now make house calls. Will attorneys be next? Lawyers may not travel to your doorstep, but for some 20,000 California BankAmericard holders, a lawyer is as close as the telephone. For a flat fee of $98 a year, participating card users have unlimited toll-free access to attorneys. Wills can be drawn up, letters issued, and legal queries answered—all without leaving one's living room.

Recently, in Florida, a special commission on Access to the Legal System recommended that the Florida Bar Assn.—representing some 26,000 attorneys in the state—"encourage the use of credit cards and other financing plans to assist clients in the payment of their legal fees." With that recommendation, the last marketing taboo was shattered.

Technically, accepting credit cards for payment of legal services has been permitted since a 1975 Florida Supreme Court ruling struck down the barrier that denied lawyers the right to split their fees with nonlawyers—in this case, 2 percent of the fee with the credit-card company. Despite the ruling, few attorneys were inclined to add credit-card machines to their office furnishings. In part, they hesitated simply because there was no compelling reason to accept credit charges. However, in today's market, where middle-income households are accustomed to paying for services with credit cards, remaining competitive requires attorneys (as well as doctors, dentists, and nonprofessionals) to conform to the expectations of the market. This is especially important for lawyers—middle-income households are the single largest market for routine legal services.

Growing in tandem with credit-card payments for legal services are prepaid legal insurance and group legal insurance. Both offer services comparable to health-insurance providers. Some 200 million Americans are covered by medical insurance, whereas only 13 million have legal insurance, although it has been available for some time. Limited advertising and consumer resistance have conspired to hold down the number of enrollees in such programs. However, legal insurance is gaining, and will continue to gain, acceptance as competition forces fees down and as consumers realize that an ounce of legal protection is better than a pound of cure.

Already accustomed to using major bank credit cards to pay doctors and dentists, many consumers soon will have in hand single-purpose medical credit cards. Medical Bankcard Corp. of Indianapolis now offers a medical expense credit card. For an $18 annual fee, consumers have available a separate line of credit for health-care expenses. The cards can be used at participating hospitals and pharmacies, as well as for the deductible and co-insurance portions of medical insurance. Said Stephen L. Taylor, president of Medical Bankcard, "VISA and MasterCard are life-style tools. We give consumers peace of mind for health-care expenditures."

An Alhambra, California, dental practice also offers patients peace of mind. The three-dentist group issues proprietary plastic allowing customers to pay for treatment "in manageable install-ments over a reasonable period of time." Dr. John Chao, the group's founder, says the card is "ideal for someone who's been putting off cosmetic or preventive dentistry for financial reasons."

The group practice has something else that few dental offices include—a full-time marketing director. Enlisted to handle patient inquiries and to publicize the new credit program, Stephen Smoke, a public relations specialist, said the plan offers the group's 3,000 patients an initial credit limit of $500. Terms include no finance charges for the first ninety days and an 18 percent annual percentage rate, about the same as most bank credit cards.

Offering single-purpose credit cards for dental services is not unique to the Alhambra group. Clinicom Management Services, a Santa Clara, California, billing service for dentists, issues a credit card accepted by four hundred California dentists. The difference between Clinicom's plan and Chao's is that Clinicom's credit is underwritten by a large finance company. Chao's group underwrites the debt itself. In 1986, consumers can expect single-purpose credit cards for legal, medical, and dental services to become widely available.

LAWYERS FOLLOW DOCTORS AND DENTISTS INTO SPECIALTY PRACTICES

American consumers have long been accustomed to being referred from specialist to specialist to treat a range of medical and dental problems. In the past few years, medical specialty clinics—health-care groups that treat one illness or group of illnesses—have mushroomed. Dental office buildings house oral surgeons, endodontists, periodontists, and general dental practitioners. More and more, consumers seeking legal advice don't go to just any attorney—they see a specialist. Along with the growth in full-service commercial legal clinics has come the development of specialized, or boutique, law firms.

Deregulation of the banking industry, for example, has created an environment in which banks require the services of lawyers trained in the subtleties of more flexible, but more complex, industry requirements. New investment accounts, new practices, and new frontiers for the nation's banks have created an area of legal specialization. Specially trained lawyers not only assist in interpreting new laws but also help banks find ways to use those rules advantageously.

As America's business community increasingly becomes integrated into the global marketplace, attorneys familiar with international law will be in great demand. Other fast-growing areas of specialization include antitrust and trade regulations, bankruptcy and collections, family law, labor law, product liability, real property law, taxation, wills, estates and probate, and workers' compensation. As the lawyer population increases and the number of legal specialists grows, attorneys offering general legal services will be forced to adopt ever more sophisticated marketing techniques to survive in a dramatically more competitive market.

TECHNOLOGY GIVES PROFESSIONALS A COMPETITIVE EDGE

Office automation is a hot market for the data communications industry (see chapter 5). In the past decade, professionals have installed sophisticated computer technology at a pace equal to that of any other business. Time spent on clerical tasks has been cut in half. In the year ahead, computer technology will simplify and accelerate the pace at which professionals conduct business.

From the small offices of independent practitioners to the multi-office and intercity complexes of private law firms, computers are revolutionizing the way attorneys practice their art. Observed Berne Rolston, a member of the thirty-two-lawyer Beverly Hills firm of Leff & Mason and chairman-elect of the Los Angeles County Bar Assn.'s Law Office Management Section: "In 1971, you would ask lawyers at seminars how many had computers, and three or four out of one hundred did. Now 90 percent do."

It is such a rapidly growing field that the American Bar Assn. and its Council on Legal Economics have set up a legal advisory council to review software made for the legal profession by 550 vendors. Available programs range from VertiSoft Corp.'s time and billing package called Ivory, designed for independent practitioners (priced at $6.95), to Matthew Bender's form wills and other documents (from $395 to $1,995).

Computerized legal research already is available through twelve-year-old LEXIS, produced by Mead Data Central, and WESTLAW by West Publishing Co. Both systems are accessible to subscribers in law firms and libraries through specially leased terminals or personal computers. The systems contain texts of state and federal appellate and Supreme Court decisions.

Teleconferencing, already used for private negotiations and conferences, soon may find application in the courtroom to eliminate costly waiting time and the expense of travel. Paperless offices where all outgoing material is kept on computers soon will be a reality, and electronic mail is making it possible to greatly reduce the amount of incoming paper. In the future, the whole of a law office's records will be accessible via the computer. Additionally, the all-important law library might one day be reduced to interactive laser-disks compact enough to store in a drawer.

Even more mind-boggling is the array of computer systems soon to be available to physicians for the identification and treatment of patients. Already physicians in some group practices store patients' medical information in portable computers shared by members of the group. When an emergency arises, the doctor on call has immediate access to the patient's medical history.

An ambitious hospital-based computer system is being developed at Cedars-Sinai Medical Center in Los Angeles, where microcomputers for on-staff physicians' private offices will be linked to computers in the hospital. Doctors will be able to check nurses' overnight reports, evaluate the results of lab tests, and take care of time-consuming paperwork without leaving their offices.

Sophisticated technology also is producing portable desktop machines that enable doctors to get test results in minutes, rather than waiting days for samples to come back from specialty labs. In an era of intense competition among doctors, desktop analyzers are becoming a multimillion-dollar business. Robert Easton, a senior consultant at Channing, Weinberg & Co., predicts that the wholesale market for diagnostic tests and testing equipment in doctors' offices will reach $250 million during 1985 and double that by 1990. About half that amount will come from clinic chemistry testing such as that run on the new desktop machines, says Easton.

So promising is the market for this new technology that it's attracting some of America's major medical equipment houses and entrepreneurs. Marketers of clinical chemistry machines for independent practitioners range from such giants as E. I. du Pont de Nemours & Co. and Eastman Kodak Co. to Electro-Nucleonics Inc., a small biomedical products company in Fairfield, New Jersey.

Boehringer Mannheim Corp., based in Indianapolis, soon will update its BioDynamics unit with a machine now sold overseas by its German parent company. And North Chicago–based Abbott Labs is poised to unveil an $18,500 machine called Vision. About the size of a microwave oven, Vision uses sophisticated laser optics and computer technology.

Although some experts caution that desktop analyzers cannot be made foolproof, and rely on the skills of their operators, competition for customers undoubtedly will put such devices in the hands of many private physicians across the country.

Computer programs also are being designed to serve as a sort of professional consultant to physicians. One such program called HELP—Health Evaluation through Logical Processing—automatically collects information about patients from medical records entered into the computer system. This record includes the patient's history and physical exam, the doctor's and nurse's notes, and data about the patient from monitoring equipment and from laboratory tests. HELP analyzes the information and asks for more information, suggests tests, offers a diagnosis or responds to the doctor's treatment plan by warning of drug interactions, patient allergies, or other potential problems.

While HELP is the first artificially intelligent computer system commercially marketed for patient care, numerous other systems have been programmed to tackle specific medical problems. ONCOCIN, designed at Stanford University, helps physicians follow complicated drug treatment programs for certain kinds of cancer. MYCIN, also a product of Stanford, helps doctors diagnose infectious diseases so that treatment can begin before all necessary information has been gathered. And ATTENDING, designed by a Yale University anesthesiologist, critiques treatment plans used in anesthesiology.

There are others and there will be more in the years ahead. Although these systems raise social and legal concerns about machines making decisions for physicians and about the danger of dehumanizing medicine, most doctors who have used them find them to be an invaluable adjunct to their practice.

What is next? Robots in the dentist's office? Probably. Robot patients with sophisticated sensory systems already allow students to probe, pick, and practice on machines that react to pain but don't suffer. Surgical robots also are becoming available.

In the year ahead, already pervasive medical technology will become more so. Soon most of us will be diagnosed and treated by a two-member team: a physician and the physician's extraordinarily sophisticated computerized assistant.

In 1986, physicians, dentists, and lawyers will confront unprecedented competitive challenges. Being a competent professional no longer will guarantee success in a marketplace dominated by educated consumers who demand quality service at affordable prices.

10 GLOBAL POLITICS MOVE TOWARD CENTER. *THE FRINGES UNRAVEL.*

Political rhetoric has given way to economic realities around the globe. Political hard-liners at both ends of the spectrum are softening their tone as countries strive to improve economics at home and achieve a competitive advantage in the global marketplace. In the year ahead, moderation will be the watchword as developed countries and third-world countries alike attempt to identify their role in what has come to be called the global economic village. Fiscal conservatism will reign. Although 1986 will mark the beginning of the end of the welfare state, social issues and personal life-style choices worldwide will assume a decidedly liberal bent.

ITALY'S COMMUNIST PARTY EMBRACES CAPITALIST GOALS

Alfred Reichlin's priorities sound vaguely familiar. He speaks of the need to reform government bureaucracy, to make the economy more competitive, to cut the budget deficit, and to encourage entrepreneurism. Not startling? These aims come from the chief economic spokesman of the Italian Communist Party—the party's acknowledged economic expert. Even more surprising perhaps is his favorable mention of Gary Hart, who interests him because of his appeal to the "new class" of technicians, professionals, and highly skilled white-collar workers, whom Reichlin sees as an essential constituent to anyone on the left.

Reichlin's sentiments are shared by others in the Italian Communist party and by Luciano Pellicani, editor of the Socialist Party's intellectual journal. In fact, left-wing party leaders across Western Europe agree that old ideas of socialism are in crisis—that conformity must give way to individual needs and values, equality to liberty. Political leaders believe that the socialist ideals are in urgent need of renovation, that socialism has lost its appeal for the young and near young who once eagerly gathered under the *bandiera rossa*—the red flag—and who are essential to continued political vitality across the board.

An even more radical policy position is the Communist Party's insistence on shifting tax burdens away from "unproductive investment" and toward investment that creates jobs. However, some "old left" postures still hold strong. Reichlin, for instance, asserts that Italy's tax and financial systems favor investors, landowners, and other "parasitical elements," with taxes falling most heavily on workers and those who invest in job-producing industry. He advocates a system fairer to both factions.

If much of this sounds eerily reminiscent of American political analyses after Reagan's second-term election, it's because Italians closely studied the 1984 election and found many of its lessons applicable. Party adversaries insist that Communists are caught in an untenable position, favoring a sort of supply-side communism while still trying to hold on to working-class constituents. They are not alone. Socialists, Republicans, and Christian Democrats are wooing Italy's young middle-class voters (Yuppies, by their definition and ours) by taking positions that are not so far removed from the Communists' new position.

Picking up votes across class lines is a priority for all parties. With 198 of the 630 seats in the Chamber of Deputies, the Communist Party already has demonstrated its ability to do so. Fabio Mussi, strategist for the party, insisted that his party was able to edge past the long-dominant Christian Democrats by "aiming squarely at the middle to upper-middle classes, women, and young people." Women's rights were cited as a principal concern, as was the environment, in a pitch to win the "green vote."

WEST GERMAN GREENS ARE ON THE RISE

Although the Greens are not widely established in Italy, West Germany's Green Party—a coalition of environmentalists, pacifists, and anticapitalists—is cited as being the greatest threat to political stability in West Germany. Disillusioned by failure to realize *die grosse Wende*—the great turnaround promised by Chancellor Helmut Kohl—young militants, hostile to the United States and opposed to West Germany's membership in the Western Alliance, are flocking to the Green Party. The party won 6 percent of the vote in the 1983 elections and captured twenty-seven seats in the Bundestag; polls indicate the Greens could win up to 15 percent in 1987 and emerge as power brokers between right and left.

West Germany's economy is far from sagging—overall growth could reach 3 percent in 1985 and be equally strong in 1986—yet there are signs of political unrest propelled by what is perceived to be an inability on the part of leadership to resolve basic economic and social problems. Voters from every walk of life complain that private enterprise is shackled by bureaucratic red tape, welfare and tax burdens, and rigid labor rules. Furthermore, scandals involving top politicians and wealthy industrialists are eroding confidence in national leaders.

Amid promises to boost private business, slash welfare subsidies, and cut tax burdens, Kohl also spoke of a moral and spiritual revival and pledged to strengthen ties with the United States and the Western Alliance. Despite the fact that he strengthened those ties, many voters have lost confidence. Even within his own Christian Democratic Party and its coalition partner, the Free Democratic Party (FDP), doubts about his leadership ability linger. (The

FDP on its own isn't a political threat to anyone. Popular support for the small centrist party is down to 3 percent. If it fails to garner at least 5 percent of the vote in the next national election, it could be ousted from Parliament.)

Perhaps Kohl's saving grace is that his principal opponent—the Social Democratic Party—is steeped in apathy, embroiled in intraparty squabbles, and rife with dissatisfaction with what many consider to be uninspired leadership by Hans Jochen Vogel.

Meanwhile, there is rising sentiment that West Germany should switch its focus from allegiance with the United States to accommodating the Soviet Union and improving relations with communist East Germany. A more balanced international posture is being pushed mostly by young and middle-aged voters whose political memory begins after World War II. As in the United States, voters and politicians now coming into leadership positions were born into an era of relative prosperity and worldwide détente, however tenuous.

Only 110 of 520 members of the West German Parliament were actively involved in World War II. The average age of Chancellor Kohl's cabinet is fifty-five: his two closest aides are forty-two and forty-four years old; most members of Parliament and the Cabinet became politically active well after the war. Consequently, pragmatism rules. In international relations, most West Germans say, sovereignty is the issue, not nationalism. They assert the country must be more self-reliant, that it must get out from under United States dominance and establish its own presence in world affairs. If that means closer ties with its communist neighbors to the east, they are prepared to establish such relations. In fact, they point to a warming trend, inspired by Russia's desire for American technology, between the United States and the Soviet Union as precedent for closer ties with East Germany.

The next two years will be decisive. If Chancellor Kohl can accomplish *die grosse Wende* he promised, the ground swell of support for the Greens may diminish, and latent anti-American sentiments will remain dormant. If not, a country already in a state of flux could face real turmoil.

FRENCH LIBERALS FIND A MODEL IN REAGAN

A dramatic intellectual counterrevolution among the French intelligentsia is a harbinger of the country's future political bent. Politically committed, left-wing intellectuals who not so long ago quoted Marx, Lenin, and Fidel Castro and supported the idea (if not the reality) of a violent revolution as the key to achieving the elusive goals of *"Liberté, Egalité, Fraternité"* are marching steadily toward the middle. Denunciations of American imperialism have given way to demonstrations against the Soviet invasion of Afghanistan, repression in Poland, and executions of political prisoners in Vietnam. They have turned their backs on communism and have embraced (much to the surprise of many) Ronald Reagan.

This intellectual about-face is particularly ironic because it coincided with the arrival in power of France's first left-wing government in over twenty-five years. But the government of Social Democrat François Mitterrand—voted into office with communist support—is no ordinary left-wing leadership. Mitterrand is committed to middle-of-the-road politics that put economics before rhetoric. Many of his economic policy positions resemble President Reagan's with a French accent. Where they depart is in Reagan's strong belief in "the magic of the market." Mitterrand prefers a more managed approach. Although he has given cautious support to liberalizing trade, he takes pains to guarantee that the pace is neither too rapid nor uncontrolled.

Mitterrand hopes to put together a new legislative majority, ranging from the moderate left to the center. He may succeed. Recent changes in voting rules will not only increase the representation of far-right and far-left parties—which thus far he has all but ignored in his effort to be all things to all people in the middle—but also strengthen the Socialist Party (minus its Communist coalition partners, who bitterly withdrew from government when Mitterrand chose an economic hard-liner as prime minister). Adopted in principle by the government, the new rules will do away with the two-stage winner-take-all elections for Parliament, in existence since 1958, and replace them with a single-vote proportional system in which seats will be distributed roughly according to each party's percentage of the total vote.

The Socialist Party is convinced that adopting a proportional system will strengthen Mitterrand's position by allowing no single party to dominate Parliament. This would open up the possibility of cooperation between Socialists and the traditional conservatives and centrists, and sustain Mitterrand through 1988. If not, say political analysts, the question of who governs France would be open to debate, leading to a potentially lengthy period of instability. Many admit France can ill afford that.

SPANISH COMMUNISTS LEARN PRAGMATISM

In Spain, political moderation is the order of the day. Today, the far right and the far left together hold less than 10 percent of the vote. "There is," writes Ian Gibson, an Irish writer on Spanish culture, "an admirable sense of pragmatism and compromise to get things right." That new pragmatism is reflected in the stripping of power of the longtime leader of the Spanish Communist Party in an effort to make the party more open and moderate. Said its secretary general, Gerardo Iglesias, "We are making the party more democratic, more dialectic, taking into account the social changes in Spain and on the left."

With good reason. The once-powerful party, crippled by infighting, won less than 4 percent of the vote in the 1982 elections and remains politically isolated by the center-left Socialist government of Prime Minister Felipe González. As in France, the intellectuals whom the party once commanded have jumped ship. Plans include ending the party's opposition to other leftist parties and allying with Socialists who are unhappy over the centrist policies of González, and with such single-issue groups as feminists, pacifists, and ecologists. Iglesias hopes to build an organized leftist opposition to the Socialists, who hold a majority in Parliament. The strategy could deny González a majority in elections scheduled for 1986, forcing a coalition.

Whatever the outcome, Spain already is experiencing a dramatic social transformation as its membership in the European Economic Community draws it closer to the rest of the continent. A political transformation is certain to follow, as young Spaniards grow into a sophisticated world of cultural attractions, chic French fashions, and open personal life-styles—all taboo under the Franco regime. Expect Spain to look and sound more like the United States and its European cousins.

SIGNS OF MODERATION IN IRAN

In the Middle East, a call for moderation is coming from some highly unlikely government leaders. Most unlikely of all: Iran's Ayatollah Ruhollah Khomeini. Although Iran still fanatically pursues its revolutionary goals, analysts detect a growing awareness among influential mullahs, officials, and top military men that new political approaches are needed to prepare for the day that the eighty-four-year-old Khomeini dies or turns power over to someone else.

Meanwhile, a debilitating war with Iraq, internal economic stresses, and deepening unrest among segments of Iran's 44 million population are prompting even Khomeini to strike a more moderate pose. Iranian officials already have told West Germany's foreign minister that Iran is willing to improve its ties with the West. In Iran, moderation also means more tolerance of the middle class. This includes merchants, many of whom resent a government run by tough clerics and according to ancient Islamic precepts, which has prevented them from trading outside their country.

China, too, is flirting with democracy, in its cautious move toward modernization. An experiment in party democracy in the central province of Shaanxi provides for election of provincial party leaders by lower-level party members in a secret ballot. However, the winners must obtain final approval from the party Central Committee.

In a separate experiment, local communist leaders in the southwestern city of Chengdu now serve a fixed five-year term of office.

This marks a dramatic shift for officials who used to serve in office indefinitely.

U.S. VOTERS SETTLE FOR MIDDLE-OF-THE-ROAD CALMNESS

The United States, however, sets the pace of this global shift to the center. If Reagan's second-term victory taught us nothing else, it confirmed the fact that Americans like their material comforts. Although Reagan's policies may not be solely responsible for the nation's steady economic growth, he was at the helm when the economy picked up, and he gets the credit.

With unemployment low, job growth high, and inflation under control, Americans are experiencing a period of calm. As in West Germany, middle-age voters with no political memory of World War II, and young voters for whom Vietnam is only a place on the map (and they're not even sure where) are planting themselves firmly in the middle of the road. Fiscally conservative but adhering to liberal personal values, voters with shifting allegiances have made party crossovers commonplace. These relatively young voters, less interested in rhetoric than in issues, are likely to abandon party politics altogether if the platform isn't right.

While concerned about world debt and growing budget deficits, most U.S. voters seem convinced that current economic strategies will work and that global economic tensions will be resolved eventually. This confidence is reflected around the globe as political rhetoric gives way to reality, bravado to bottom lines.

FREE ENTERPRISE SPREADS AROUND THE GLOBE

The spirit of free enterprise, which has long characterized America's internal economic development and international economic policies and is enjoying a rebirth in a phenomenal entrepreneurial boom, is spreading. Western Europe has enthusiastically embraced the concept, in practice if not in policy statements. Asian countries are instituting capitalist-style work incentives and permitting at least a partially free market. In fact, communist rulers almost everywhere are adopting free-enterprise practices to shore up their faltering economies.

In the Soviet Union, Mikhail Gorbachev's emphasis on greater productivity through modernization has prompted a Politburo directive to start teaching computer technology to students in secondary schools. An urgent need to go on-line countrywide, in order to remain competitive with Western technological societies, will do more to warm trade and political relations between the U.S. and Russia than any number of summit meetings.

Russia hopes to follow in Hungary's footsteps, now emerging as the Soviet bloc leader in software exports. In broadening its private-sector economy, Hungary has carved a niche in Western Europe for its software products, which range from computer games to sophisticated software control programs. One-third of Hungary's software output comes from small, privately owned companies. Many consist of one or two computer buffs and an outdated machine.

JOBS RISE IN U.S., FALL IN EUROPE

Entrepreneurism is the engine that drives America's economy and is largely responsible for the creation of over 15 million jobs during the last decade. In that same period, Western Europe suffered a net loss of 2 million jobs, forcing widespread and, to date, intractable unemployment. In 1970, Turkey was the only European country with double-digit unemployment; now Britain, Belgium, Denmark, Italy, Ireland, Portugal, and Spain share that dubious distinction. France may join them. Only a handful of countries, notably socially conscious Sweden and Austria, oil-rich Norway, and Luxembourg and Iceland (which have small populations), have kept unemployment low, frequently by subsidizing troubled businesses.

Virtually every European country and many non-European nations hope to mimic America's extraordinary success at job creation by sharply reducing disincentives to hire or be hired when unemployed. (In 1986 we are almost certain to see the beginning of the end of the welfare state.) These countries are learning to capitalize on weakened union power, institute job-creation schemes, endorse entrepreneurism, and support small-business development.

For decades, Western Europe has stood almost united in its defense of workers and its support of an array of social benefits and job security rules that far exceed anything the United States government offers. Now indications are that European leaders are questioning the wisdom of such policies and are actively reversing decades-old policies. In Britain, Prime Minister Margaret Thatcher refused to budge when coal miners went out on strike to sustain nonproductive mines. Some mines have closed, others will follow. Denmark's coalition government withstood a bitter, sometimes violent, three-week general strike and held wage increases down enough to lower workers' standard of living by 2 percent. Across the continent, government leaders are letting corporations slip through loopholes in existing tough labor laws—and in some cases creating the loopholes themselves.

In France, for example, heads of all nationalized industries except steel were told that their jobs were at stake if the companies did not end the year in the black. To achieve that goal, they were allowed to fire workers—a socialist no-no for decades. Mitterrand's appointment of Georges Besse to head the ailing Renault auto company is indicative of a willingness to stand for hard-nosed capitalistic tactics to revive a depressed industry. Previously Besse had taken over the money-losing, state-owned Picheney, a chemical company, and made it profitable by lopping off several divisions and persuading unions to go along with job eliminations.

France, too, is pioneering efforts to infuse entrepreneurship into the economy without destroying the fabric of social welfare laws. Weakening such laws, however, is a very real next-step possibility. Several years ago, France offered newly unemployed people the option of taking generous unemployment benefits in a lump-sum payment. The government's hope was that many dismissed workers would start their own businesses. Many did. Called the "capitalization of unemployment benefits," the program has since been copied by many Common Market countries. Considering that in the Netherlands, unemployed workers receive between 75 and 99 percent of their last salaries, one-time lump-sum payments guarantee considerable start-up capital.

Despite the unions' weakening power base, as a result of dwindling membership and waning public and political support, France remains hesitant to go too far against the grain of unions. Strikes have ended inconclusively, often in complete failure, as with Britain's coal mines. Unlike German and Scandinavian unions, which are more pragmatic and enjoy a close working relationship with industry and government, internecine struggles and politicization divide French unions and are almost certain to diminish their power even more. Throughout Europe, with the exception of West Germany, unions are losing membership and with it their strength.

While labor laws remain sacrosanct in most countries, some nations are beginning to narrow their scope. Spain and Belgium, for example, have given companies an extended grace period during which they can dismiss newly hired young workers without enduring expensive red tape or paying the huge unemployment compensation involved in firing older workers. Several countries have frozen minimum wages and even permit companies to pay below-minimum wages to young workers. Holland and Belgium no longer tie wages to inflation. France, Holland, Denmark, and Germany cut social benefits slightly, and Britain has reduced payroll taxes a bit.

DECLINE OF THE WELFARE STATE

Evidence that the welfare state is on the decline is apparent in declarations made by officials in Sweden—long the leading symbol of western Socialism. Tough measures were necessary there, officials said, to prevent deterioration of Sweden's balance of payments and to bolster international confidence in the national currency, the krona. Sweden has been infected by the political and economic conservatism that influences much of the rest of Europe. Political leaders who argue that the welfare state must be trimmed have gained considerable support. Pledges to lower taxes—the highest in the industrial world—and to open government services such as day care and medical care to private competition have given increased support to the Moderaterna party, the most conservative of the non-Socialist parties, particularly among young voters who resent the bureaucracy of the welfare state.

Probably the clearest indication of shifting attitudes is a new pro-business posture that makes heroes of entrepreneurs as well as captains of industry. This attitude is being adopted around the globe. In a joint statement issued at the close of the seven-nation economic conference in Bonn, in May, the represented countries—Britain, Canada, France, Italy, Japan, West Germany, and the United States—declared they would "work to remove obstacles to growth and encourage initiative and enterprise so as to release the creative energies of our peoples while maintaining appropriate social policies for those in need."

Britain already has moved in this direction. By eliminating the salary ceiling on which employers pay a 10.45 percent national insurance tax, British officials have made it more expensive to employ higher-salaried workers. The move is expected to generate more than $910 million toward a program to reduce insurance charges for lower-salaried workers and the self-employed. The overall effect is intended to encourage entrepreneurs and make it cheaper for large businesses to hire unskilled workers.

LOOSENING STATE CONTROL OVER ECONOMY

Most surprising of all are the number of communist countries that are adopting free-enterprise practices to shore up their faltering economies. One communist country after another is relaxing total state control of the economy, as a variety of experiments are introduced that have little in common with the goal of centralized planning and even less with the teachings of Marx or Lenin.

In China state-owned enterprises are now authorized to issue stocks and bonds to raise funds. Dividends are paid to worker-shareholders. Additionally, wide autonomy in the manufacture, distribution, and pricing of consumer, industrial, and agricultural products has been granted to the country's state-owned enterprises. Hungarian officials openly admit they are moving away from the traditional Marxist goal of total social equality, with the result that the nation enjoys the highest standard of living of any of the Soviet bloc countries. And new laws in Yugoslavia require factories that are chronic loss takers to reduce wages to the legal minimum. Even the Soviet Union, most resistant to free-market reforms, now allows some service industries to keep any profits they earn as the winds of change blow through this bastion of communism.

In an effort to revitalize a limping economy and invigorate a sluggish industrial work force, Poland has endorsed entrepreneurism. Some 650 privately owned companies, most financed from abroad, have cropped up in Warsaw in the last three years. Although these companies, all involved in light manufacturing such as clothing and cosmetics, account for no more than 1 percent of Poland's national production, they are being increasingly viewed as the cutting edge of efforts to shore up Poland's economy.

Who's next? Cuba and Vietnam. Fidel Castro is upending economic practices in place since communist rule began in 1950. Factory managers are being encouraged to circumvent central planners in Havana and work out deals with each other. In Vietnam, capitalist-style work incentives and a partially free market have been gaining increased support from the Marxist regime. Entrepreneurs are being granted permission to open their own small factories, providing they do not employ more than fifteen workers. Although heavily taxed, most consider it worthwhile.

Also in Vietnam, land on state-owned cooperatives has been divided among families—the larger the family, the larger the plot of land—and anything they produce, beyond their contract allotment to the state, they may sell.

ANIMOSITY GIVES WAY TO ECONOMICS

If politics makes strange bedfellows, economics makes even odder ones. Traditional adversaries are making conciliatory gestures, and new alliances are being formed, in efforts to improve positions in world trade markets.

A 1,007-room $75-million luxury hotel in Peking stands as an architectural testament to international joint ventures around the globe. Owned jointly by an American company, the E-S Pacific Development and Construction Co., and the state tourist monopoly, the China International Travel Service, it will be under the management of the ITT-owned Sheraton chain. The project represents the largest single investment involving American interests since Deng Xiaoping and his fellow reformers in the Communist Party reopened China to foreign equity holdings six years ago.

So far, only thirty Chinese-American enterprises have been undertaken, with a total capitalization of $100 million to $150 million, but Deng is committed to opening China to foreign trade and investment.

The Deng government also has legitimized trade with its old adversary, South Korea. Begun in secrecy in the 1970s, trade is now carried out in the open, with ships sometimes sailing directly between the two countries. Estimated at up to $800 million annually, trade has smoothed the way for government-to-government contacts. Political analysts, encouraged by the trend, assert that warmer relations between Peking and Seoul portend improved relations between North and South Korea. That remains to be seen.

China also has reached agreement with Indonesia to begin normalizing relations between the two longtime antagonists. The agreement put an end to eighteen years of official silence between them. Indonesia broke relations with Peking after an abortive communist coup in 1965 that Indonesia accused China of backing. Now Indonesia hopes to increase non-oil exports to China to compensate for falling world oil prices.

Peking is poised to reclaim land that once was part of China: Hong Kong. In an agreement reached with Britain, Hong Kong will be turned over to China in 1997—the most massive negotiated turnover of a noncommunist population to communist control since France agreed to pull out of North Vietnam.

Can communism and Western capitalism coexist in a tiny colony devoted to free enterprise? That question is being asked throughout the world. Chinese leaders in Peking say they can. Chinese residents of Hong Kong are not quite so optimistic. But as China relaxes trade policies with partners across the sea, chances of a successful merger increase.

U.S. interest in the Pacific Rim countries is growing rapidly. In fact, exports and imports between America and Pacific Rim nations outstrip U.S. trade with Western Europe. Investment from Japan in America exceeds $50 billion—nearly ten times what it was just fifteen years ago—and investment by U.S. business interests in Japan is as high and growing just as quickly (see chapter 2). Although Japan continues to be criticized for exploiting foreign markets while tightly controlling its markets at home, business activity is lively in both directions.

With the world's fastest-growing economy, Pacific Rim countries are quickly becoming international trade mission targets. Even South Korea has strengthened ties with Japan, its onetime colonial master. Japan remains attractive to investors, but China runs a close second as it opens its trade doors a little wider. One of China's strongest attractions for foreign marketers is its one-billion-plus population—the world's largest consumer market. Said Lloyd Vasey, president of Pacific Forum, a Honolulu-based think tank, "The center of gravity has already shifted in business, trade, and investments. It [the Pacific Rim] is where all the action is going to be."

The Pacific may not be where all the action is—but it will get a lot of it.

LIFTING THE COMPUTER BAN

Technology will be the great equalizer in global politics. Already, the Soviet Union is negotiating to buy large numbers of Western-made personal computers, including Apple and IBM models. The move comes at a time when Soviet scientists are complaining about their country's faltering efforts to build its own microcomputers, resulting in personal computers being smuggled in. Executives at computer firms approached by the Soviets say Russia may buy tens of thousands of computers for schools and research projects, from vendors in Britain, France, West Germany, and Japan, and, if trade restrictions are relaxed, from the United States.

Those restrictions may well be relaxed. In a potentially significant concession to exporters, the U.S. Commerce Department has proposed new regulations that permit products to be exported if the exporter can show that similar goods from other industrial countries are available in "comparable quality and in such quantities that controlling them would no longer improve United States national security."

Computer manufacturers would have no difficulty doing so. IBM and Apple will soon be speaking Russian.

Signs point to a willingness on the part of Reagan and Gorbachev to establish a good working relationship. While neither seems willing to abandon a circumspect posture, both speak of the need to keep momentum going in the global economy. Without at least lukewarm trade relations, that momentum cannot be maintained for long.

GROWTH OF THE GLOBAL ECONOMY

In general, the international outlook is bright. In the year ahead, fewer references will be made to "domestic economies," as acceptance grows worldwide that the global economy is the only economy.

Debts carried by the less developed countries still linger as a threat to global economic stability. But steady improvements in Brazil and Mexico, and promises by Argentina, Venezuela, and Uruguay and other nations to exert tighter controls on spending at home, suggest there could be light at the end of the tunnel—however long that tunnel might be. Meanwhile, global economic interdependence has brought enormous gains in living standards, diet, and health care in the industrialized countries and appreciable progress in much of the developing world. Many newly emergent countries already play a major role in worldwide trading networks.

Over the past few decades, many barriers to international trade in goods have been dismantled. Consequently, citizens around the world enjoy a wide choice of domestic and foreign goods that are often cheaper or of better quality than available previously. The next major hurdle is freedom of choice in services: banking and finance, architectural work, insurance, consulting and transport services, among others. A first tentative step has been taken in an agreement reached by the ninety member nations of the General Agreement on Tariffs and Trade. Each country has agreed to conduct a study of its own service industries and trade in services —conceivably the beginning of a global financial/transportation/general services industry.

THE 10 BEST PLACES TO START A BUSINESS

INTRODUCTION

A year of reading daily local newspapers and traveling around the country has led us to discover that a number of places are making every effort to encourage entrepreneurial enthusiasm and support small businesses. We've selected ten that head the list of terrific places to start a business.

Other areas that might well have made the list if it were longer include: Raleigh, North Carolina; Loudon County, Virginia; Sarasota, Florida; New Hampshire, Vermont, and San Jose. San Antonio can hardly be included without mentioning Austin. The same is true of St. Petersburg and Tampa. However, in our estimation, the ten places named below are truly outstanding locations in which to launch a business.

ANN ARBOR, MICHIGAN

Ann Arbor is well on its way to becoming a robotics center for the United States (see chapter 1). Radiating out from the University of Michigan (UM), world renowned as a first-class center for research and development, companies large and small are feverishly automating the automobile industry, and finding new applications for robotics technology. In 1986, a 500-mile strip labeled Automation Alley—beginning in Ann Arbor, stretching north to Detroit and south to Cincinnati—will gain international recognition for advancements in factory automation and mass production of technology-based consumer products.

Several Michigan communities provide an attractive environment for entrepreneurs, but Ann Arbor stands out. Even when the state's economic outlook was bleakest, Ann Arbor held a firm course. Population and economic growth were slow and steady. UM was, and is, a strong magnet for high-tech entrepreneurs. Start-up companies seeking a foothold in Ann Arbor often find the university to be both customer and facilitator.

Ann Arbor's vibrancy can be attributed to economic diversity and a commitment to getting products out of the research and development stage and into the marketplace quickly. Perhaps the single most important component of Ann Arbor's strength is the public and private sectors' conviction that small businesses are the area's economic heartbeat. Aided by state government, this city offers entrepreneurs an extraordinarily well-developed support system.

The Chamber of Commerce, in cooperation with two state development agencies and the federal Small Business Administration, has created the Chamber Innovation Center to "help budding new entrepreneurs turn their ideas and inventions into successful new businesses by providing most of the necessary new business needs."

Also available to entrepreneurs in Ann Arbor (and throughout the state) is the Michigan Technology Council's Business Plan Review Forum. The Forum "provides an organized opportunity for entrepreneurs to receive business, technical, and other advice from several appropriately experienced individuals."

Across Michigan, small businesses benefit from the state's commitment to economic development. With Governor James J. Blanchard leading the parade, Michigan is marching steadily out of its slump. Noted Governor Blanchard: "We've cut out taxes for small business, but we haven't cut taxes for big business in Michigan. That's not to say I wouldn't like to, but our priority is small business."

In 1982, Michigan passed a law allowing up to 5 percent of its public-employee pension funds to be used as venture capital. With $450 million under management, the state is one of the nation's biggest venture-capital firms. A strategic fund has been created to distribute up to $40 million each year in loans and grants to help companies adapt new technology. Much of that money will go to small research and development firms working on software programs, machine-vision systems, and robotics.

Michigan is a state on the rebound and Ann Arbor is its shining light. A cooperative relationship between business and state government promises to make Michigan an even better place to work and do business.

ATLANTA, GEORGIA

Atlanta and Georgia have a problem other places wish they had: growth. Georgia's population has grown by 374,000 people since 1980, making the Peachtree State the fourth fastest-growing state. Of some 50,000 new Georgia residents in 1984 alone, more than half settled in metro Atlanta.

Atlantans on the whole are relatively wealthy (although pockets of poverty in the city and surrounding county cannot be ignored) and well educated, making Atlanta an ideal market for consumer goods and services. Georgia has led all fifty states in personal income growth since the second quarter of 1982. The state's employers added almost 178,000 jobs in 1984, a growth rate of about 8 percent. More than half that growth was in Atlanta, which added a record 98,700 jobs.

Atlantans also are young—the median age in 1980 was 28.9 years —and internationally sophisticated. As this Southeastern hub moves into the second half of the decade, it will become a center of international trade and development. Foreign-based companies increasingly choose Atlanta as their U.S. headquarters. Some 229 foreign companies have based U.S. operations in Georgia, most of them in Atlanta.

Asked why they chose Atlanta, most firms cite the proximity to fast-growing Southeastern markets and easy access to Hartsfield

International Airport. Some 70 percent of the U.S. is within a two-hour flight, and regularly scheduled flights to Europe and Canada carry international marketers directly to their home cities. A thirty-three-acre Foreign Trade Zone adjoining Hartsfield allows the movement of foreign or domestic goods without going through U.S. Customs.

Georgia actively lures foreign businesses, with Atlanta as bait. The state has trade and investment offices in Athens, Brussels, Hong Kong, Oslo, Seoul, Tokyo, and Toronto. The Georgia Department of Industry and Trade maintains an international division to assist foreign companies interested in operating there. Atlanta offers the World Trade Club, where visitors meet leaders of Georgia's international business community. And a growing number of law, architectural, engineering, and accounting firms specialize in services to international companies. Atlanta also is well on its way to becoming an international financial service center.

Georgia is committed to excellence in education. More than half of the state's public expenditures are for education. Georgia Tech, recently awarded $21.3 million to help the Pentagon develop sophisticated computers for its Star Wars program, the University of Georgia, outstanding in biotechnology research and development, and Emory University, earning a reputation for biomedical research, are among the state's thirty-seven senior colleges and universities. The Advanced Technology Development Center makes the state's technological resources available to high-tech industries, helps companies market new technology-based products, and provides "incubator" space for product development groups or start-up firms. The $30 million Georgia Research Consortium pools education and private-industry resources to accelerate high-tech research and development.

Atlanta is fast becoming a repository for venture-capital funds. In the last two years, the availability of funds has increased from a sprinkle to a shower of money. In September 1982, there was less than $5 million in locally managed venture capital. Today the figure is over $150 million. The emergence of locally based capital pools came at a critical time for the area's infant high-tech industry. While high tech has been around for a while, most Atlanta firms involved in technology were large companies. But these large companies have begun to spin off new ventures, many started by former employees. They had expertise, good ideas, but no funds.

Now they have money and Atlanta's high-tech industry is on the move.

CONNECTICUT

Connecticut is all business about small business, offering exceptionally well-developed support systems for people interested in starting companies. Small business accounts for half the state's annual gross product of $45 billion, and 80 percent of all jobs created. In June 1984, recognizing the contribution small businesses make to the economy, Governor William O'Neal signed legislation creating the Connecticut Small Business Advisory Council, designed to encourage development of a strong small-business sector.

The Connecticut Department of Economic Development serves as the hub of an extraordinary wheel radiating out in all directions. Financing for new product development is available through the Connecticut Product Development Corp. Businesses, start-up ventures, and entrepreneurs can get up to 60 percent of eligible development costs to turn innovative ideas into products and processes. Low-interest loans for new or existing manufacturers or wholesale distributors are available through the Small Manufacturers Loan Program. Low-cost, long-term financing is available from the Connecticut Development Authority to help companies with capital expansions. Managerial assistance is provided by the state's Small Business Office.

Connecticut is one of twenty-three states that did not wait for the federal government to approve Urban Enterprise Zones. Six Connecticut cities—Bridgeport, Hartford, New Britain, New Haven, New London, and Newark—offer investment incentives to manufacturers, commercial businesses, retailers, and residential property owners undertaking new capital investments. Export assistance and sales leads assist manufacturers selling or looking to sell their products overseas. State firms also are matched with overseas companies interested in undertaking joint-venture projects and licensing agreements. Department offices in West Germany and Japan provide international links, and trade missions are undertaken annually to drum up new international business.

Connecticut entered fiscal year 1984 in its best shape in sixteen years. A surge of business expansion and new business growth kept unemployment well below the national average. Venture-capital funding soon will be available through a \$20-million public–private pool. And the General Assembly recently approved a \$17-million High Technology Initiative, at the same time creating a Connecticut Technology Assistance Center to assist high-tech entrepreneurs.

With Yale and forty-nine other colleges and universities providing an educational infrastructure, Connecticut's labor force is well-educated and prepared for the challenges of the information age.

INDIANAPOLIS, INDIANA

A remarkable renaissance prompted *The Wall Street Journal* to name Indianapolis "the star of the Snow Belt." An open dialogue between the public and private sector has fostered a strong partnership that enhanced the city's economic development efforts.

Indianapolis's rebirth began with Uni-Gov, a 1970 state law that merged the city and a large segment of Marion County under a consolidated government. As a result, Indianapolis now ranks fourth nationally for lowest state and local taxes on personal income, 23 percent below the national average in local government debt, and 28 percent below the national average in per capita government operating expenses. Uni-Gov also quadrupled the city's land area to almost 370 square miles, boosted the tax base from less than a half million to almost three-quarters of a million residents, and decreased government operating organizations from forty-six to six.

Public-private cooperation was responsible for the Hoosier Dome, a 61,000-seat stadium that is home to the former Baltimore Colts and the centerpiece of Indianapolis's growing amateur and professional sports complex. Other projects funded through public–private resources include Union Station, a full-scale entertainment complex, and White River State Park, an urban waterfront activity center with its first phase—the Indianapolis Zoo—scheduled to open in late 1986.

The Hoosier Dome and the Colts attract almost as much attention (but not quite) as the Indianapolis 500. Market Square Arena is home to the National Basketball Association's Indiana Pacers. Along with becoming a professional sports mecca, the city is developing a reputation as a major amateur sports center. Several world-class facilities have been built, including the Indianapolis Sports Center, site of the annual U.S. Open Clay Court Tennis Championship; a top-rated natatorium which hosted the 1984 U.S. Olympic diving, swimming, and synchronized swimming trials; a banked concrete velodrome for major cycling events, and an all-weather track and field stadium.

But Indianapolis isn't just for sports enthusiasts. The combined campuses of Indiana University-Purdue University at Indianapolis (IUPUI) boasts the country's second-largest medical school, an extensive medical center, and research facilities known for work in robotics, biotechnology, and other high-tech fields. IUPUI is home to the Indianapolis Center for Advanced Research, whose goal is to "provide specialized technology and perform exploratory, advanced and engineering development to enhance the economy of Indianapolis and Indiana."

Committed to developing a nurturing environment for small business, Indiana has incorporated the entire state into one Certified Development Corp. for the Small Business Administration's 503 programs. The Indiana Employment Development Commission has loan guarantee authority for approximately $80 million, as well as an extended guarantee program from a $60 million state account. Following in the footsteps of a handful of states, the General Assembly passed enabling legislation for the Indiana Business Development Credit Corp. This program, like similar ones in other states, allows financial institutions to pool credit for small business loans.

Venture capital is increasingly available to start-up companies in Indianapolis. The Venture Club of Indiana, located in Indianapolis, helps put entrepreneurs in touch with venture capitalists.

The Indiana Small Business Council hosts an annual conference on small-business issues, and the Indiana Institute for New Business Ventures offers a broad range of services for small and emerging businesses. Among them is the Indiana Emerging Business Forum, which offers entrepreneurs a chance to present business proposals to experts who can offer advice on management, capital availability, and business expansion.

Only a sampling of the powerful network available to entrepreneurs, these programs are evidence of government leaders' commitment to new business. Private business leaders also are involved in new business development through the Indiana and Indianapolis chambers of commerce. Indianapolis is determined to maintain its newly earned image as the star of the Snow Belt.

MASSACHUSETTS

In his state-of-the-state address, Governor Michael S. Dukakis commented that "the thriving economy of Massachusetts has given government and business the chance to offer work to everyone, spur a resurgence in communities and reach out with expanded human service programs." He assured residents that the new era is "not an elusive, Utopian dream," but would be built on the base of a "pulsating economy driven by high technology and entrepreneurs, and supported by government programs." Governor Dukakis has every reason to be optimistic, and people with an entrepreneurial drive have every reason to consider Massachusetts as a place to do business.

Massachusetts is education, innovation, and Yankee ingenuity. Just a decade ago, it was a run-down industrial state, struggling with layoffs and plant closings, with a jobless rate higher than any other major industrial state. Today Massachusetts's employers have difficulty finding people (not just skilled workers, but workers at all levels) to fill the 140,000 new jobs created in 1984—many of them created by 40,000 new businesses started in the past two years. The state enjoys one of the lowest jobless rates of any state, 3.8 percent. (Interestingly, only six states ended 1984 with unemployment levels lower than 5 percent. Just one was in the Sun Belt—Arizona—the others were Massachusetts, Connecticut, Rhode Island, New Hampshire, and Vermont.)

Leading an economic revival that is turning New England into one of the U.S.'s most prosperous regions, Massachusetts shows big gains in business start-ups, service jobs, financial services, and construction activity. And, of course, central to its economic vitality is high technology. Virtually every state is searching for a way to hitch its wagon to a high-tech star; Massachusetts has done it. At least one-third or more of the 400,000 jobs created since 1975 have been in technology-related businesses.

Boston, the state's leading high-tech and all-around success story, is by no means the state's only community to benefit from a high-tech explosion. Brockton, Fall River, Lawrence-Haverhill, Lowell, New Bedford, and Pittsfield all rank electronics and electronic machinery among their top three manufacturing groups. In fact, Lowell has come to symbolize community rebirth.

The existence of computers and state-of-the-art data communications capabilities helped turn Boston into a financial service center. Even greater growth in the financial service industry is being experienced in Boston's suburbs. Several critical factors—a first-class educational network, excellent transportation facilities, and access to world markets—make banking, investments, accounting, and insurance the largest private contributors to Boston's economy.

But the state's greatest strength comes from its entrepreneurial drive, supported by a small-business infrastructure that is continually being improved upon and plenty of venture capital and traditional financial resources. In 1983, Massachusetts financiers controlled 13 percent of U.S. venture funds—more than $1.5 billion.

Massachusetts has many of the same programs Connecticut and Indiana offer in support of small-business development, and is equally committed to creating an environment in which public–private partnerships flourish. Massachusetts also provides an information and assistance network for small businesses interested in exporting. The Massport Small Business Export Program (SBEP), in conjunction with the Small Business Association of New England, operates a unique international marketing service.

Project Export, a one-year trade program partly funded by a grant from the U.S. Department of Commerce, expands the scope of the SBEP. Small and medium-sized businesses will be introduced to new markets in the Far East, Latin America, and West Africa. In addition, to encourage international trade, Massachusetts has designated part of Logan Airport and Pier 51 as Free Trade Zones.

To maintain its competitive edge Massachusetts wholeheartedly supports research and development efforts through a variety of tax breaks and educational training and development programs. State officials have found a way to harness its most precious natural resource—people—and is committed to keeping the entrepreneurial spirit alive.

MESA, ARIZONA

When most people think Arizona, they think Phoenix or Tucson. But soon, they'll think Mesa, too. Fifteen miles west of Phoenix, Mesa catches some of the spillover from Phoenix's extraordinary growth. Arizona's third-fastest growing city, at 10 percent annually, Mesa is on its way to becoming a center for conventions, tourism, technology corporations, and retailing activity.

If one word were used to describe Mesa's business climate, that word would be dynamic. The population is well educated and the labor force highly skilled. Industry has been moving to Mesa, attracted by its excellent climate and well-managed growth. Major employers in the area include Hughes Helicopters, Talley Industries, Empire Machinery, General Motors, Cox Newspapers, Motorola, National Semiconductor, and Rogers Corp.

Lower costs attract conventioneers to Mesa's 3,000 hotel rooms (none of which costs more than $100 a night). Recognizing the hospitality industry's impact on economy, a Convention and Visitors Bureau was formed. Recreational facilities bring return business.

Mesa has planned carefully for growth in area as well as in population. In the late 1970s, for planning purposes, city officials identified future boundary limits and began to follow a careful program of annexing land within this area. Mesa's heart, the Town Center, underwent a $40-million face-lift in 1983, financed by private enterprise. That renovation sparked rebuilding efforts in every direction. Since then, $85 million has been invested in the Town Center, $75 million of it from the private sector.

In the last decade, 6,000 new businesses have set up shop in Mesa, attracted by a friendly and cooperative attitude among local officials. Manpower training and nearby educational facilities, offering laboratories and research and development agencies, add to Mesa's attractiveness as a place to start business.

Equally important is Arizona's pro-business posture. Business inventories are exempt from property taxes and no corporate franchise tax is imposed. Furthermore, Arizona has focused its efforts to diversify and expand its economic base not only on attracting high-tech businesses (as have others), but on creating an investment climate in which Arizona-based businesses can flourish.

Phoenix is booming and Mesa benefits. This is not to say that Phoenix is not a good place to start a business (it is), but for someone seeking a less-developed area, with all the big-city amenities, Mesa stands out.

MINNEAPOLIS–ST. PAUL, MINNESOTA

Minnesota is small business—in many cases small, home-grown businesses, earning million-dollar profits and creating satellites that circle the earth. And the state intends to remain small business. Minneapolis and St. Paul are attractive hometowns for many new businesses. Among the Twin Cities' lures for business is the University of Minnesota, whose Institute of Technology offers pioneering programs in control systems, heat transfer, biomedical engineering, and microelectronics. Scholars from the institute helped start forty-four new biomedical companies in the state.

Minnesota is committed to excellence in education at all levels. A state-operated foundation program has gone a long way toward equalizing dollars spent on education between rich and poor counties. Minnesota also holds the distinction of having the lowest high school dropout rate. Consequently, its labor force is well prepared to take on the challenges of the information age.

In 1958, a one-year-old company, without its first order, was running out of cash and financial backers were in short supply. Bob Zicarelli, an investment analyst, convinced a friend at Allstate Insurance Co.'s investment department to fly to Minneapolis and check out the struggling company. His friend did. Three years later, the company, Control Data, captured the imagination of Wall Street. Allstate's $700,000 investment was worth nearly $50 million.

Control Data's success clinched the Twin Cities' reputation as one of the nation's important high-technology centers. It also set the area apart as a leading market and source for seed money for entrepreneurs. According to Venture Capital Journal, Minnesota ranks among the top ten states in availability of seed money. In 1982, for example, Minnesota ranked sixth in new start-ups funded by venture capital.

Control Data, with William Norris at the helm, helped create the Minneapolis mystique—a reputation for aggressive, innovative business management, enhanced by a determination to improve the social condition in every community it touches. Part of that mystique, too, is the spin-off phenomenon. High-tech giants attract entrepreneurial employees, who, having honed their skills in the corporate cradle, spot a market niche and fill it. What's more, companies here encourage spin-offs. Employees from Sperry Univac begat Control Data. Control Data spun off Cray Research, Data Card, Network Systems, and Data 100. People from Data 100 created Lee Data and Laserdyne.

And then, of course, there is 3M. Years ahead of current corporate lore, which holds that companies should create a nurturing environment for entrepreneurs, 3M began pursuing that policy. Minneapolis–St. Paul—in fact, the state of Minnesota—are better places because of it.

An open dialogue between government and business has earned Minnesota a reputation for fostering dynamic leadership in both arenas. High state taxes would be expected to discourage business investment; they haven't. Minnesota residents demand, and get, top-notch civil and social services and expect to pay for them. That the tax burden is equitably distributed makes it easier to swallow.

Minnesota's economic base is diversified. High-tech industries are strong and growing stronger. Financial services are a growing sector of the state's economy, with two of the nation's largest bank corporations—Norwest and First Bank Systems—based there. Employing 115,000 workers, the insurance industry is a major factor in the state's economy. Agriculture remains important, as does manufacturing.

While virtually every community in Minnesota welcomes new firms, Minneapolis–St. Paul provides a superb environment for business starts. Although Minnesota's agriculture and mining industries remain depressed, nonfarm employment spurted 7 percent in the fourth quarter of 1984, and retail sales surged 28 percent. Most of that growth occurred in the Twin Cities.

The Twin Cities posted a 19 percent gain last year in construction employment, and both downtowns are thriving. St. Paul has completed more than $1 billion worth of development in the past seven years. Growth will continue. The Minneapolis Federal Reserve Bank expects retail sales to increase 8.5 percent by the end of 1985, and nonfarm employment will increase about 5.7 percent. Not bad for a state and city often covered by a thick blanket of snow. Minneapolis–St. Paul winters may be colder than many others, but they're hot towns in which to do business.

SAN ANTONIO, TEXAS

In 1980, San Antonio became the tenth-largest city in the country. The city has never looked back. Once notable for a progress-inhibiting rift between its impoverished Mexican-American community and its privileged middle- and upper-income families, it is earning a reputation for cooperative government and unity among its residents. Symbolic of this hard-won unity is the Target '90 Commission. Composed of twelve task forces, encompassing citizens from all sectors—government, nonprofit agencies, neighborhood groups, and education—the 500-member commission has responsibility for setting goals for San Antonio to reach by 1990.

Some of the goals identified by the commission are not surprising—better education, an ensured source of water, and better fire and police protection. But others exemplify the city's innovative spirit and ambitious determination. Convinced, as was everyone, that technology would carry it into the twenty-first century, San Antonio set out to win its piece of the pie. Efforts have paid off. The city now boasts several computer component manufacturing plants and its very own teleport.

Aware that Austin to the north was in a stronger position to attract computer-related research and development interests (largely because of the University of Texas), San Antonio contented itself with being a site for the production of computer components —terminus of a silicon corridor stretching seventy-five miles between the two cities—and as a center for research in medicine and bioscience. Today, it is emerging as a first-class center for biotechnological research and development. San Antonio's extraordinarily popular mayor, Henry Cisneros, courts both computer firms and major pharmaceutical houses.

San Antonio is sprucing up, as commercial development reaches new heights. The city's well-known Riverwalk is being extended to include a $140-million center for offices, hotels, and a large shopping facility. Some $27 million will be spent to expand the San Antonio Convention Center. Restoration of the Aztec Theatre includes a new concert hall, residential condominiums, and retail space.

The retail industry is buzzing. Builders Square, a chain of warehouse-type home-improvement stores to be operated by K mart, will be based in San Antonio. Publishing giant Harcourt Brace Jovanovich soon will open a 141,000-square-foot plant, and Control Data will increase its presence in the city with 265,000 square feet of manufacturing space.

Alive with anticipation, encouraging growth and development wherever possible, San Antonio will benefit from the state's growing interest in creating an environment responsive to the needs of small businesses. Two new legislative initiatives have been put in place to support start-up firms. Tax-free revenue bonds will finance projects for both established and start-up firms through the Texas Small Business Industrial Corp. Aid soon will be available to agricultural and other processing facilities, also through tax-free bonds.

Capital, venture and otherwise, is increasingly available to Texans with an entrepreneurial inclination and the drive to see it through. Two years ago, only five or six Texas venture capitalists were active; today there are about forty-five. Operating primarily out of Dallas, venture capitalists go where the ideas are. And to a large degree, that's San Antonio.

SAN DIEGO, CALIFORNIA

By 1995, San Diego County will be the second largest county in California. The city of San Diego is prepared for growth—in fact, anxious to accommodate newcomers by pursuing a flexible growth-management course.

A downtown skyline that barely existed a few years ago now is littered with construction cranes. Hampered by a low (10,000) core-city population—not particularly attractive to retailers and other service providers—the San Diego City Council created Centre City Development Corp. (CCDC) in 1975 to implement an extensive redevelopment plan. A major goal was to attract 50,000 more residents by the end of the century. To accomplish that, the city set aside blocks of land for residential development. With millions of dollars being poured into commercial construction, offices, shops, and restaurants, San Diego became an even more attractive place to live and work.

Diversity describes San Diego's economy. Once dependent on military expenditures for its well-being, the city now boasts a mix of business activity. Said Max Schetter, senior vice-president of the San Diego Chamber of Commerce and director of economic research: "Our economic base is more sunrise- than sunset-oriented. Our industrial makeup is growing and has a bright future as local companies expand and as new industries are attracted to the San Diego area."

Among those new industries are health sciences and biomedicine, largely due to the presence of the University of California-San Diego; Scripps Clinic, the nation's oldest and largest center for research, teaching, and public service in the marine sciences; the Salk Clinic, and others that have created a nucleus for that industry. As the industry grows, it spins off entrepreneurs who take innovative ideas and bring them to market.

Jobs in high-tech manufacturing more than doubled between 1972 and 1982, increasing at an average annual rate of 7.6 percent, as compared to a 2.3 percent growth rate for other categories of manufacturing employment and a 2.4 percent rate for high-tech manufacturing nationwide. Approximately four hundred electronics firms are located in San Diego County. Everything is in place for San Diego to emerge in the next few years as one of the top three areas in the country in technological developments.

Retail activity has reached an all-time high. Although Northern California is geographically larger, Southern California generates 60 percent of the state's retail sales. Three counties—Los Angeles, Orange, and San Diego—contribute 80 percent of all Southern California business activity. San Diego County, with a buying income in excess of $20 billion, produced almost $11.7 billion of 1983 taxable sales.

San Diego is among the state's top five counties in tourism revenues. Tourism generated nearly $1.4 billion in 1983, accounting for 5 percent of the county's gross regional product of $28.8 billion—a 7.3 percent increase over 1982. To boost tourism revenues even higher, the city is undertaking a massive promotional effort to make San Diego a major West Coast cruise port. And the city is fast becoming a major convention center.

Silicon Valley attracts more attention, but Southern California is the new target for venture capitalists tired of competition up north. Venture capitalists based in Southern California raised $209 million in 1983, more than ten times the amount available in 1982. Southern California in general, and San Diego in particular, have the crucial components necessary for entrepreneurs to flourish—venture capital, along with accounting, investment banking, marketing, and advertising support.

San Diego's growth—population and economic—is expected to be above statewide levels this year. Local government and business leaders are enthusiastic about that growth, but continue to emphasize management and judicious development to maintain San Diego's extraordinary quality of life.

TAMPA, FLORIDA

The Tampa Chamber of Commerce Committee of One Hundred introduces business people to the city by proclaiming it is the only "Megatrend city" east of the Mississippi. And so it is. What made Tampa a Megatrend city four years ago makes it a terrific place to start a business today.

Tampa is one of the fastest-growing cities in the U.S. Outstanding quality-of-life advantages, a warm climate, an excellent economic outlook, a diverse and abundant labor supply (one-third of Florida's population resides within 100 miles of Tampa), and fast, convenient access to all major markets create a magnet for corporate headquarters.

A downtown resurgence unequaled in Florida is turning Tampa into a "twenty-four-hour city." It's anchored on the south by Harbour Festival Island's festival marketplace and convention center, which flag wavers say will cement Tampa's national reputation and reap millions of dollars, and to the north by the performing arts center, expected to spark renewed development in that area. Built in response to repeated queries about the city's cultural offerings, from business executives interested in relocating there, the performing arts center provides Tampa with cultural clout. The convention center, on the other hand, will attract business and economic development.

Tampa is moving into the international marketplace. The Port of Tampa, conveniently located for exporting to the Caribbean Basin, also is the closest deep-water port to the Panama Canal. A substantial number of international dollars already are invested in Tampa and surrounding Hillsborough County, through twenty-two foreign-owned and -operated corporations located there. The firms employ 1,500 Tampa residents, with an annual payroll of $22 million. Recent trade missions to Canada were reported to be promising.

Local government and business leaders, through the Mayor's International Trade Fair Advisory Committee, are working together to attract international business by marketing Tampa's Free Trade Zone. Tampa has an active International Trade Council, formed with the goal of establishing the city as a center for international trade. An equally important feature is Tampa's multilingual community, providing international firms with a cultural mix from which to recruit executives.

Financial center of Florida's west coast, Tampa serves as regional and national headquarters for several banks and insurance companies. Corporate and small business loans are readily available from the city's financial community.

And finally, with a rich supply of firms in science and technological industries, Tampa is emerging as a major research and development center. Located near the University of South Florida, which provides laboratories for research, ongoing employee education, and scientific talent, Tampa's technology "corridor" has access to abundant support systems for high-tech start-up firms.

Businesses that need to reach out and touch someone, anyone, anywhere in the world will benefit from one of the most advanced cable and fiber-optics communications systems, just getting under way. Tampa plans to be a vital, economically sound member of the global economic community in the twenty-first century. It's well on its way. Although controlling growth has become Florida's number-one legislative objective, Tampa is not likely to slow its development pace—only temper it with some carefully laid plans.

INDEX

NO POSTAGE
NECESSARY
IF MAILED
IN THE
UNITED STATES

BUSINESS REPLY MAIL

FIRST CLASS PERMIT NO. 14025 WASHINGTON, D.C.

POSTAGE WILL BE PAID BY ADDRESSEE

The Naisbitt Group
P.O. Box 25536
Washington, D.C. 20007